T0316567

Cambridge Elements ☰

Elements in Current Archaeological Tools and Techniques
edited by
Hans Barnard
University of California, Los Angeles
Willeke Wendrich
University of California, Los Angeles

MOBILE LANDSCAPES AND THEIR ENDURING PLACES

Bruno David
Monash University

Jean-Jacques Delannoy
EDYTEM, Université Savoie – Mont Blanc

Jessie Birkett-Rees
Monash University

COTSEN INSTITUTE OF
ARCHAEOLOGY AT UCLA

CAMBRIDGE
UNIVERSITY PRESS

Shaftesbury Road, Cambridge CB2 8EA, United Kingdom

One Liberty Plaza, 20th Floor, New York, NY 10006, USA

477 Williamstown Road, Port Melbourne, VIC 3207, Australia

314–321, 3rd Floor, Plot 3, Splendor Forum, Jasola District Centre, New Delhi – 110025, India

103 Penang Road, #05–06/07, Visioncrest Commercial, Singapore 238467

Cambridge University Press is part of Cambridge University Press & Assessment, a department of the University of Cambridge.

We share the University's mission to contribute to society through the pursuit of education, learning and research at the highest international levels of excellence.

www.cambridge.org/BDavid
Information on this title: www.cambridge.org/9781009467797

DOI: 10.1017/9781009181594

First published 2024

A catalogue record for this publication is available from the British Library

ISBN 978-1-009-46779-7 Hardback
ISBN 978-1-009-18158-7 Paperback
ISSN 2632-7031 (online)
ISSN 2632-7023 (print)

Additional resources for this publication at www.cambridge.org/BDavid

Mobile Landscapes and Their Enduring Places

Elements in Current Archaeological Tools and Techniques

DOI: 10.1017/9781009181594
First published online: March 2024

Bruno David
Monash University

Jean-Jacques Delannoy
EDYTEM, Université Savoie – Mont Blanc

Jessie Birkett-Rees
Monash University

Author for correspondence: Bruno David, bruno.david@monash.edu

Abstract. This Element presents emerging concepts and analytical tools in landscape archaeology. In three major sections bookended by an Introduction and Conclusion, the Element discusses current and emerging ideas and methods by which to explore how people in the past engaged with each other and their physical settings across the landscape, creating their lived environments in the process. The Element reviews the scales and temporalities that inform the study of human movements in and between places. Learning about how people engaged with each other at individual sites and across the landscape deep in the past is best achieved through transdisciplinary approaches, in which archaeologists integrate their methods with those of other specialists. The Element introduces these ideas through new research and multiple case studies from around the world, culminating in how to 'archaeomorphologically' map anthropic constructions in caves and their contemporary environments.

Keywords: archaeomorphological mapping, created environments, reconstructing past landscapes, temporality of place, caves and rockshelters

ISBNs: 9781009467797 (HB), 9781009181587 (PB), 9781009181594 (OC)
ISSNs: 2632-7031 (online), 2632-7023 (print)

Contents

1 Introduction

Archaeologists often study the past through individual objects, sets of objects and specific locations – 'artefacts', 'assemblages' and 'sites', as they are conventionally called. In reality, however, people live out their lives in much broader spatial settings. Those broader settings involve many environmental features, people, plants, animals and other worldly beings, all of which are known, and connected, through culture. These culturally known and experienced places are the landscapes of people's lives.

Understanding those past landscapes is the stuff of archaeology, which does so through the material remains people left behind. Archaeology does not have a monopoly on how to historicise the present, for there are also other ways of knowing and imagining the past, but in this Element we focus on how the material record can be interrogated through scientific methods. If archaeology is a practise of historicism concerned with understanding what people did, and how people were, in the past through their material remains, then 'landscape archaeology' refers to the study of any or all dimensions of the broader spatial contexts through that material record. This includes how places may be meaningful in different ways to different peoples or cultures – *how* people relate to things is precisely what creates a distinctive material (archaeological) record. It is this meaningfulness that makes archaeology able to study the material traces of cultural practices through time. 'Archaeology sits in places', Kisha Supernant (2022) recently wrote in homage to Keith Basso's (1996) *Wisdom Sits in Places*. People and place are thoroughly intertwined and mutually defined. Landscape archaeology is the study of all the things that reveal aspects of that intertwined spatial history through the particularities, organisation, patterns and trends of material culture – the biographies of material life, which we may think about as *material behaviour*. This Element concerns how we can archaeologically investigate how people engaged with places through time while also moving around the landscape. These investigations are applicable at a range of scales, from examinations of extensive, regional settings to studies of the localised landscapes created within sites.

In archaeology as elsewhere, 'space' is not abstract but culturally constructed. This applies both to the ways that people in the past created the landscapes of their lived experiences and to the ways that archaeologists choose to analyse types and dimensions of space, such as in the way we structure an area conceptually into types of landforms, or the choice of measurements and grid units used in analyses. 'Placial' is how philosopher Edward Casey (e.g. 1997, 2001) prefers to call these constructions of the place-world, for in the kinds of work that archaeology does, they are cultural places first. This Element aims to decipher those cultural dimensions of how people constructed, engaged in and engaged across their place-worlds through time, across a range of spatial and temporal scales.

With such a broad remit, there are also very many ways in which cultural landscapes can be read from the material record, and they can relate to a vast array of past human practices. In about 30,000 words, this Element cannot do justice to every method, every case study or every topic that landscape archaeology covers: it is not an exhaustive review of the literature (for discussions of the English landscape tradition that has been particularly influential in Anglophone archaeology, see, e.g. Fox 1923; Hoskins 1954; Johnson 2006; Schama 1995). Instead, we present three essays that strategically target emerging concepts and analytical tools, especially as they relate to the archaeology of mobility and temporality of the landscape (Section 2), the geomorphological reconstruction of past environments (Section 3) and caves and rockshelters as built places (Section 4). While the Element is not a manual of field techniques, Section 4 outlines how to archaeomorphologically map one particular kind of enduring place recurringly used as people moved across the landscape – caves – as a way to investigate their human engagement.

Throughout this Element we use some common terms for which our uses require definition to avoid confusion. Prominent among these is 'occupation', which we use not just to mean a residential base but, in the sense of Tim Ingold (2000) and Julian Thomas (2008), also 'dwelling' and 'inhabitation'. Using a place in a specialised way, be it for religious rituals, the extraction of raw materials, for a passing encounter, for trade, as an arena of conflict or in any other way, means that the place in question was 'occupied' through its engagement.

We also differentiate between the different kinds of chronological ages that archaeologists and other Quaternary scientists use. 'Years ago' refers only to calendar years before the time of writing, for us in this Element being the year 2023 CE. Raw (uncalibrated) radiocarbon ages are conventionally presented as 'BP' (before present), meaning radiocarbon years before calendar year 1950 CE. Calibrated radiocarbon ages are presented as 'cal BP', referring to converted calendar years before 1950 CE (sometimes they are calibrated as 'cal BCE' or 'cal CE' to make them fit the Gregorian calendar). Throughout this Element, we have calibrated radiocarbon ages on Calib 8.20 using the IntCal20, SHCal20 or Marine20 curve depending on the type of material and source location of the dated sample, and present calibrated ages at 95.4 per cent probability (2 sigma). 'BP' and 'cal BP' only refer to uncalibrated and calibrated radiocarbon ages, respectively; no other kind of chronometric age uses 'BP' (the reason being that the concept of 'BP' and its calibrated version 'cal BP' automatically embeds the entire set of assumptions and provisos that specifically comes with radiocarbon dating). Other kinds of chronometric dating, such as optically stimulated luminescence (OSL) and uranium-series (U-series), also use 'years ago', and are usually given relative to the year of their measurement (unless otherwise stated in their original publication) – working out the year of reference for any such reported age can be difficult, because sometimes in the original publications such ages had been standardised for comparability with radiocarbon ages, and therefore converted relative to 1950 CE, but this is not always the case. We do not use the abbreviation 'ka' to refer to thousands of years in the past, because we have found that in the literature the use of 'ka' often masks inconsistencies when comparing ages from multiple sources. This is particularly problematic when researchers have used chrono-metric age databases ('big data') to find patterns and to model colonisation pathways, demographic trends, patterns of intensification and the like. Rarely is each and every chronometric determination traced back to its original publica-tion to work out whether each age is suitable for the task at hand (including assessing each dated sample's depositional and taphonomic status). This is a huge problem, as in such applications all kinds of chronometric ages are typically used without knowing exactly what their limitations are (see also Ward & Larcombe 2020). We have closely examined the ages recently used in a number of regional studies, and in most cases found that their reporting as 'ka' has mixed different kinds of ages (e.g. radiocarbon, OSL, U-series and of varying chronostratigraphic reliability) without entirely working out which are really reliable first (despite some attempts to do so), for to do so would require careful re-reading and re-assessment of the details of the dating in their original reports, and therefore take much preliminary (but not insurmountable) work first.

We stress that as the years pass, the temporal space between calibrated radiocarbon ages (relative to 1950 CE) and the now of 'years ago' increases, so that it may not matter for something that is tens of thousands of years old. But the already and growing seventy-three years difference between 1950 and the now of the time of our writing (2023), or even more of our reading, often does matter for something that is Late Holocene in age. Adhering to the conventions of chronometric nomenclature, such as the differentiation of 'BP', 'cal BP' and 'years ago', avoids this problem – and indeed this is precisely why those conventions were designed in the first place. Furthermore, we think it is important also to not lose sight of the scale and experience of human time when discussing human history: 35,000 years gives a much better sense of the enormity of the time scale, and of the generations of ancestors involved, than 35 ka. It presents a different kind of meaningfulness, one better appreciated in human time scales. Writing archaeology is not just about the past; it is also about telling stories that are meaningful in the present. We are influenced here especially by the Indigenous communities we work with and learn from.

1.1 Seven Key Principles

In the work of archaeological excavation, it is not unusual to return day after day, week after week and sometimes year after year to the same site as one excavates progressively deeper into its accumulated deposits. Digging a few millimetres at a time with small trowel in hand, our eyes and all our senses are finely attuned to what is gradually revealed from the underground: the contents, structure and taphonomic indicators of buried deposits. But this brings a conundrum: the sites we investigate need to be looked at in well-focused, myopic detail, and yet understanding those same sites also requires a scalar retreat, a consideration of the longer distances in which the site is located. This is because each site formed under broader contexts: social and cultural, geomorphic, biogeographic and climatic. Of course, archaeology is not just about digging; it involves a wider-ranging set of studies, including field surveys that are more readily cognisant of that broader scale. But the work of understanding that wider-ranging landscape in which a site formed, was added to and transformed through time requires more than archaeology. It needs also the attention of a whole raft of specialists who are trained to ask questions about, and to read the signs of, the formation processes that made the site what it is today.

The first key principle we thus wish to highlight in this Element is that doing landscape archaeology extends beyond the expertise of archaeologists. It requires working with geomorphologists, biogeographers, cartographers, chemists, Quaternary geochronologists, cultural knowledge holders (in many places Indigenous), surveyors and related geomatics (spatial sensing, analysis and data storage and communications) specialists, among other disciplinary practices, in *transdisciplinary research*. Here we differentiate between multidisciplinary, interdisciplinary and transdisciplinary approaches. Multidisciplinary research typically occurs when different specialists apply their knowledge and skills to address multiple dimensions of a general topic, such as when archaeologists investigate the deep-time history of a site and pollen analysts examine its vegetation history, but where the two narratives are largely their own. Interdisciplinary approaches are more coordinated, with team members each investigating a shared research question using specialist skills and knowledge, such as when archaeologists try to understand how the distribution of stone artefacts across the landscape corresponds with the distribution of raw material sources by working alongside geologists. Transdisciplinary approaches are even more integrated, referring to where two or more disciplines rupture each other's limits by adding new knowledge and methods into the internal workings of each, so that the whole is greater than the sum of the parts. An example is the concept of 'archaeomorphology', explored in Section 4. It refers to where archaeologists, geologists and geomorphologists combine their disciplinary skills to work out how people engaged with their surroundings to socially engineer their geomorphic environments. We think that transdisciplinary research is the most powerful way to resolve questions that are bigger than those typically asked of single disciplines. The case studies discussed in the following pages demonstrate this point.

The second key principle is that places accrue the traces of the past through time: what happens at one time is prelude to what takes place next. This cumulative process can be thought of as a 'building perspective' (McFadyen 2008), the elements of which can be disentangled archaeologically by 'reverse engineering' the material evidence. Such an approach requires working out the fine details of the material record so as to construct a *chaîne opératoire* or operational sequence for how places were engaged in the past and through time (see Section 4).

The third key principle is that the methods we use are constantly developing, so that tomorrow we will, or should, be able to do things we cannot today. We have therefore chosen to write about the archaeology of mobile landscapes and their enduring places through emerging methodological know-how. The case studies discussed in the following sections cite analytical methods that are beginning to shed light on past landscapes in ways not possible even just a few years ago. In some cases, the ideas can now be explored because the new methods allow us to think in new ways. An example is our ability to work out through archaeomorphology how caves were actively constructed to suit the cultural purposes of the time, as elucidated in Section 4.

The fourth key principle relates to *scale*: understanding deep-time historical landscapes requires good dating and good spatial differentiation. This means lots of dates and fine-grained spatial data. But *many* dates does not mean *any* dates: as archaeological scientist and geochronologist Anita Quiles (personal communication 2022) often stresses, *date what you should, not what you can*. Spatially, the data need to be commensurate with the questions asked, and vice versa (e.g. Linse 1993; Lourandos 1996). The sections in this volume each address this issue of scale in their own, varied ways.

The fifth key principle is that *the details matter*. To get the 'big picture' we first need to get the specifics – the details – right. Otherwise the house of cards falls down as we come to realise our overgeneralisations and mistakes, and if we don't, the house just wobbles in the face of contradictory patterns and data, sometimes without quite knowing where that wobbliness comes from. Or worse, we become fooled by our own fictions, and the science becomes myth.

The sixth key principle is that in many parts of the world the 'archaeological' sites and landscapes are Indigenous homelands. Often Indigenous peoples are knowledge holders of the past cultural practices undergoing archaeological investigation. That knowledge may relate to specific practices and meanings, or it may relate to the cultural frameworks in which those practices were embedded. When researching ancestral Indigenous cultural practices, the best kind of archaeology is an ethical one done not just with the permission or even in collaboration with Indigenous Traditional Owners, but also in partnership, so that every aspect, including formulation of the research aims and questions, methods, personnel, production of results and conditions by which the research is undertaken, is worked out in fully informed mutual accord. Indigenous peoples are often specialist experts of cultural knowledge, descendant community members with ethical rights to their own culture and heritage. In cases where there are no Indigenous Traditional Owners, there are almost always local communities for whom the landscape is home. These communities, too, are knowledge holders, but of a different kind, with their own interests in the material records of the past and their own questions informed by their experiences of the landscapes they live in. Archaeologists may only be present for a few weeks or months of the year, but local people know the places undergoing research in all seasons and over extended periods of time, such that seasonally exposed sites or artefacts are familiar and the recent past and local significance of places are well known. Collaboration and sharing of knowledge in these settings is a true benefit to landscape archaeology as well as being an ethical approach in which archaeology can serve community interests. This may also mean that sometimes doing archaeology, or asking a particular question of the archaeological record, may simply not be culturally and ethically tenable and therefore may not be apt.

Last but not least, we strive to *explore ideas in new ways*, and *extend our thinking through new ideas*. Stay in the comfort of where we are and all we will see is what's already in front of us, what we already know. Each section in this Element tries to look at the archaeology of mobile landscapes and their enduring places – spatial histories – in new ways, and to look at new things. We try to shift our conceptual glance, even if sometimes the emerging methods are just beginning to shed light on new ways of doing things.

2 Moving across the Landscape: The Temporality of Place

— landscapes, like time, never stand still

(Bender 2002:S103)

Seen as a fixed point in time, the archaeological record appears static. But the events and engagements that took place to create the archaeological record occurred through connections that people made across the landscape, and through time. Concepts of time and movement are thus integral to the study of archaeological artefacts, sites and landscapes, in their formation, in the ways that people engaged with them, and in how today we interpret the past through methods and concepts that reach us from all corners of the globe. It is these dimensions of time, movement and connectivity that we address in this section.

2.1 Time and the Archaeological Landscape

In archaeology, time is discoverable in the landscape by considering the ways that the archaeological record formed. Fundamental to this is the layering and juxtaposition of the material evidence, which was produced at various times in the past, and of the durations of the human activities and elemental forces that produced that material record. Time in the archaeological landscape is in this way present as sequential, 'chronological' time, but also as a record of events of different durations. These interpretations each relates to a notion of time as a successive past, present and future that can be identified with various social and environmental processes. Time is also relational, as archaeology involves the subjective and situated experience of time: the temporality of place, and of the past, can be read and perceived from the material record. The approaches that researchers take to interpret the temporal dimensions of that record affects how past lives, events and site formation are understood.

How time has been gauged by researchers over the years – *through* time – has shifted and diversified. Geoff Bailey (1981, 1983) was one of the first to specifically address the temporal properties of landscapes, taking in chronologies, dating and site formation processes, but also considering connections between past peoples' experiences of time and archaeologists' perceptions of time. The concept of time and its articulation in archaeology, in terms of duration and scale, has more recently received detailed attention in Gavin Lucas' (2005) *The Archaeology of Time* and in his more recent reassessment, *The Archaeology of Time Revisited* (Lucas 2021), and in several edited volumes (e.g. Holdaway & Wandsnider 2008). Oliver Harris' (2017, 2021) work explores issues of assemblages and scale relevant to multi-temporal landscapes, and Rachel Crellin's (2020:chapter 3) review of the theoretical issues of scale and change succinctly addresses the contrast between measured time and experienced time. This recent attention on time builds on a long history of conceptual and applied work on this topic in archaeology (e.g. Bender 2002; Ingold 1993; Knapp 1992; Kubler 1962; Renfrew 1981), which has seen the development and refinement of methods for determining chronologies, and a diversification of concepts by which archaeologists investigate time from the archaeological record.

2.1.1 The Time of Phased Archaeological Sequences

Linear sequences of time are typically one of the first ways that archaeologists learn to think about relationships between time and the archaeological record (Lucas 2005:114; Murray 2008:170; Witmore 2007:197). This approach arranges the temporality of the archaeological record into chronological sequences of discrete or overlapping periods defined by specific types of artefacts or sociocultural settings. The sequencing of stratigraphy as time was inspired by both the eighteenth-to-nineteenth-century geological works of James Hutton and Charles Lyell, and Enlightenment notions of social progress that were influential in the emerging disciplines of the social sciences, such as history, philosophy, sociology and anthropology (as evident, for example, in the works of Auguste Comte, Karl Marx, Herbert Spencer and Lewis Henry Morgan; see e.g. McGlade 1999:144). This way of thinking about time as linear sequence reflects the empirical need to provide archaeologists with a unifying framework to arrange and compare differences in the material record, such as stone artefact types or faunal assemblages (Bailey 1983:67; Ingold 1993:157; Kubler 1962:72). Using such frameworks to study change in the archaeological record, many archaeologists have pigeonholed and named individual eras (e.g. 'Early Bronze Age') or archaeological 'cultures' (e.g. the Yamnaya) into set blocks of time, each of which can have its own internal temporal dynamics, rather than discuss the archaeological record through the continuous timelines implied by radiocarbon or calendar ages, for example. Establishing phased time may be useful as a way of classifying, but it also brings its own challenges, not the least of which is the problem of what happens when we get a phase category wrong, carrying with it erroneous attributions of associated sites, materials and conceived landscapes.

This notion of time as phased is also manifest on the ground through the vertical sequence of stratified sediments from successive periods. Those sediments represent *buried landscapes*, beneath the present surface. Typically, increasing vertical distance below ground equals increasing temporal distance from the present. Chronological information can be established by arranging layers into relative sequences of depositional or erosional events from oldest to youngest. By reference to oral histories and remembered pasts, historical documents, seriation or by employing scientific dating techniques, more or less precise and accurate calendar ages can be determined for the window of time in which an artefact was used or a place was occupied. Bayesian modelling has provided a tool for combining (e.g. radiocarbon) ages relating to specific locations down a stratigraphic profile with further independent temporal details such as stratigraphic provenance or information on the relative phase of associated artefacts, to refine the ages of chronological

sequences (see Link 1, available as supplementary material at www.cambridge
.org/mobilelandscapes). Chronological phases, relative sequences and chronometric dating establish the temporality of material culture, providing archaeologists with a means to discuss issues of process, duration, contemporaneity or succession in the material record of the past and across the landscape.

2.1.2 The Shifting Pace of Time

An abstract view of time as a container (think of the named archaeological 'cultures' or 'periods'), a measure or a vector of social change, does not allow for the different speeds at which events or social changes can take place (McGlade 1999:42; Vavouranakis 2015:36). The need to address issues of scale and type of time has prompted researchers to divide and reframe monolithic, sequential time into the multiple temporalities of events and processes. This shift in thinking about relationships between time and process builds on ideas developed in the French *Annales* school of history, founded by Febvre and Bloch in 1929. They critiqued established models of 'event-centred history' (*histoire événementielle*; Simiand 1903), arguing that social change is driven by the intersection of processes active over a range of time scales. Fernand Braudel subsequently advanced a model of time in which history and social change are structured by processes active at three analytical scales: short-term sociopolitical events and 'the individual' (*événements*); medium-term, social or cultural fluctuations that take place over several decades (*conjonctures*); and the *longue durée* of socio-historical and environmental processes occupying centuries and millennia (Braudel 1972:20). The scale of the *longue durée* describes human society in relation 'to the environment … in which all change is slow, a history of constant repetition, ever-recurring cycles' (Braudel 1972:20). The notion of the *longue durée* has been particularly influential in archaeology, especially that of cultures without writing where the lives of individuals have been more difficult to decipher. This three-fold division of time provided a structure by which archaeologists could think about the cumulative effects of social and environmental processes operating in a range of temporal rhythms.

The integration of temporal, spatial, material and behavioural dynamics in Braudel's approach, translated into English in 1972, resonated with ideas current in 'processual' archaeology at the time (e.g. Clarke 1972; Renfrew 1972). The adoption and development of the *Annales* approach by archaeologists was particularly pronounced in the 1980s and 1990s, although it was not embraced equally by all the different branches of archaeology (Barker 1995; Bintliff 1991; Knapp 1992). Many relevant examples can be found in Mediterranean research, especially John Cherry's surveys of the Greek islands of Melos and Keos (Cherry 1982, 1983; Cherry et al. 1991) and John Bintliff's (1991, 1997) investigations of fluctuating urban and rural populations in Boeotia, Greece. In such studies, conducted at the scale of regional landscapes, archaeologists considered a range of temporal rhythms in their explanations of social change over time.

The consideration of multiple temporal scales for the study of human history provided new options for landscape archaeology. Longer-term time scales (durations) were initially seen as appropriate for smaller spatial scales (covering larger areas, with less detail), and so archaeological studies of broad areas were most commonly associated with the *longue durée*. Indeed, Bailey's (1983) initial investigation of time in the archaeological record considered the *longue durée* to be the most appropriate for archaeological study. An implication of this outlook was the perception that investigations of the archaeological landscape, at smaller spatial and longer temporal scales, could only result in broad (time-averaged) snippets of past social trends rather than achieving highly detailed vignettes. Also, the structure of the *longue durée* addresses and privileges environmental variables, resulting in the problematic implication that cultural behaviours are determined by their associated environmental contexts. *Landscape* archaeology, in this figuration, often privileged and became con-founded with visions of *environmental* archaeology. Approaches to time in the archaeological landscape needed to be more dynamic than the Braudelian system: the human past is not necessarily limited to the short term, medium term and long term, like the second hand, minute hand and hour hand on a clock. The need to consider how time was lived, experienced and perceived in human activities, and the importance of studying intersections and connections between events and processes operating at different temporal scales (Lucas 2021:52–53), prompted further inspirations for how to think about time in the archaeological landscape.

2.1.3 Temporalities and Seasonalities

Questions of temporality in the interpretation of the archaeological record had previously come to a head in the 'Binford–Bordes' controversy of the 1960s and 1970s. This debate questioned what sequential changes in Mousterian stone tool assemblages meant for how Neanderthals behaved across the landscape. French archaeologist François Bordes (1953) had divided Mousterian stone tool assem-blages into four distinct types identified on the basis of morphological styles. He interpreted each assemblage type to be roughly contemporaneous but to have been made by a different Neanderthal cultural group, each with its own, distinctive lithic tradition: stone artefact style = cultural group. Lewis and Sally Binford disputed this interpretation, arguing instead that Bordes' four assemblages were in fact one, with the differences in tool types relating to differences in stone tool function (Binford & Binford 1966). This was a debate about style versus function, but it also signalled a broader shift in the ways that archaeologists approached the archaeological record, with culture-historical approaches such as the one employed by Bordes being challenged by the processual and behavioural concerns of the New Archaeology that was then emerging, especially in the United States. The debate continued into the 1970s and early 1980s, with adjacent chapters presented in Colin Renfrew's (1973) *The Explanation of Culture Change* (Binford 1973; Bordes 1973; see also Binford 1982), and remains relevant in the discipline today.

The particular relevance of the Binford–Bordes controversy for our discussion of time in the archaeological landscape is the temporality involved in the interpretations. On the one hand, Bordes' argument relied on distinctive cultural groups of Neanderthals producing distinctive stone tools that came in and out of the archaeological record over very long time frames. The underlying implication is that Neanderthal subcultures themselves endured over tens of thousands of years. On the other hand, for the Binfords, the chronostratigraphic variability of the artefact assemblages implied differences in the types of tools used in the *seasonal* use of the landscape. These differing interpretations of temporality have direct implications for our understanding of mobility across the landscape, for the endurance of sociocultural practices and for the formation of enduring places to which people come and go within and across generations, and return, through very long time frames.

In their interpretation of seasonality, the Binfords were strongly influenced by ethnographic accounts of seasonal variations in the tool kits of individual cultural groups, in particular the Wik Mungkan of Cape York Peninsula in northern Australia, as reported by Donald Thomson (1939), and Lewis Binford's own work with the Nunamiut of Alaska (Binford 1978, 1980). Informed also by Michael Ascher's (1961, 1962) ethnoarchaeological studies of site formation processes, Lewis Binford did not consider the material record studied by archaeologists and ethnographers to be equivalent, nor that their interpretative goals could be equivalent, for 'the archaeological record [is] an ordered consequence of levels of adaptive organisation which are difficult to appreciate directly through the observation of events and episodes in the "quick time" perspective of the ethnographer' (Binford 1981:197).

2.1.4 The 'Pompeii Premise', Palimpsests and 'Time-Averaged' Deposits

This leads to a second important debate precipitated by an article in which Lewis Binford (1981) interrogates the scales of time that archaeologists can, in his view, productively investigate. Binford's paper was written in response to work by Michael Schiffer (1976), a student of Binford, in which Schiffer had suggested that Binford and others working in New Archaeology approached the archaeological record under a 'Pompeii premise'. This refers to the idea that the archaeological record is a captured moment in time (Ascher 1961:324), where artefacts are found essentially left as they were last used, and that 'inferences are possible only when one's site has yielded Pompeii-like assemblages' (Schiffer 1985:18). In turn, Binford then accused Schiffer of failing to appreciate the active role of site formation processes on the archaeological record. The 'Pompeii premise' debate essentially questions how archaeologists should interpret events and behaviours from the material record, especially in mixed or disturbed deposits. Where Binford saw the formation processes of the archaeological record as requiring study at longer temporal scales, Schiffer sought for the events that occurred at shorter temporal scales.

The 'Pompeii premise' rests on the idea that an archaeological deposit has remained largely undisturbed by later actions or events. In practice, the processes producing archaeological layers rarely result in intact spatial configurations of event-related artefacts and chronostratigraphic sequences. In some sites, distinct event horizons of accumulated materials can be distinguished, while in others multiple depositional events have become aggregated into compound horizons. Archaeologists have developed well-defined vocabularies to convey the degree to which an individual depositional event can be differentiated within an archaeological deposit. The most established is the concept of *palimpsest*, borrowed from manuscript studies and inspired by the work of historian Frederic William Maitland (1850–1906), in which a 'palimpsest' describes a page on which recent text is superimposed over partially erased earlier writing (Crawford 1953; Hoskins 1954). The earlier text is still present in differing degrees and has various points of contact with the more recent text. These multiple, ancient texts are therefore not past, but simultaneous and present, just as multiple archaeological materials deposited over time can overlay and intersect one another at a site and in the landscape. These more or less combined traces from different periods may also be given new roles, values and meanings over time (Renes 2015:403). The 'palimpsest' of mixed materials from different activities and time periods is often referred to as a 'time-averaged' deposit. This term usefully draws attention to the processes of deposition, removal and mixing in the formation of the record, but may also give a misleading impression of equal emphasis on all processes, durations or periods represented in the deposit (Bailey & Galanidou 2009:218).

In order to understand how the multi-temporal landscape has developed, and to work out the actions and events that formed the archaeological landscape, we need to recognise the human and environmental processes active on sites and artefacts. After deposition, materials are subject to processes of accretion, erosion and reuse, resulting in uneven preservation and visibility of the archaeological record. Understanding site formation processes is also important to decide on appropriate research questions, analytical techniques and the reliability of conclusions that might be reached (LaMotta & Schiffer 2005:91). Michael Schiffer (1987) and Reid et al. (1975) have presented a framework for thinking about site formation processes and artefact histories, outlining the stages which most objects go through on their way to forming an archaeological deposit, such as procurement, manufacture, use, deposition, decay, reclamation, reuse and recycling (LaMotta & Schiffer 2005:92). Although these stages are presented as a linear sequence, each stage can also be thought of as a node that mediates between an active or 'living' context and its surviving archaeological expression (Aldred 2020:8). Archaeological objects, sites or landscapes may move back and forth numerous times between the different stages. For example, a stone can be extracted from a quarry, worked into a tool, used, kept and curated over time, and then discarded on the ground. Years later it can be picked up again and reworked and reused.

In determining the sequence and duration of the events that produced such artefacts, sites or landscapes, the concept of *chaîne opératoire* is relevant. This analytical approach reverse-engineers from the end product the technical processes and social acts involved in the step-by-step production, use, discard and reuse of artefacts. This is most commonly applied to stone tool manufacturing technologies, but can also be applied to the formation and engagement of any part of the archaeological landscape (see Section 4 for examples of its application to whole sites as enduring nodes in the landscape).

2.1.5 The Temporality of the Landscape as Constructed in Social Time

We have seen that time can be viewed as an abstract frame used to arrange the archaeological record, and it can be viewed as operating at different speeds and scales depending on the particular processes in question. Another way to think about time is as a social construction. Archaeological interest in the ways that time can be perceived, imbued with meaning and experienced by people has led to the consideration of an array of socially and culturally meaningful 'temporalities' (Vavouranakis 2015:35). Where chronological *time* is quantifiable and supposedly neutral, *temporality* instead relates to the experience of the passing of time through a sequence of lived or experienced events. These temporalities, and this relational notion of time, can be related to human activities that have particular social schedulings, cultural understandings, temporal durations and spatial extents, such as the daily, embodied experience of moving with a herd of animals from a dwelling to a pasture, or the time it takes to build something one step at a time, or the scheduling and duration of social activities spread over a season or year.

The ways that archaeologists think about time, and the ways these ideas are applied to the study of the archaeological landscape, need not be in opposition (see Harris 2021). Linear chronology retains a central role in archaeology, allowing the relative timing of changes in human societies to be distinguished and understood and for connections between archaeological and environmental records to be made at multiple geographical scales. The formation of the archaeological record clearly relies on sequences of articulating processes and events, providing scaffolding on which to build histories and narratives of sites and landscapes. But interpretations also benefit from attention to the experiences of people in the past, of different cultural understandings of time and the multiple temporalities of human activities that produce the archaeological landscape. As Tim Ingold notes, 'the landscape ... unfolds the lives and times of predecessors who, over the generations, have moved around in it and played their part in its formation' (Ingold 2000:189).

2.2 Dynamic Landscapes: Moving from Place to Place

Mobility is generally understood as a complex phenomenon intrinsic to all societies (Aldred 2020; Murrieta-Flores 2009), a position that expands on the early work of Gordon Childe (1950, 1958) on human migrations, Lewis Binford (1980) and others on settlement and subsistence, and more recent investigations of the embodied experience of being in the landscape (e.g. Hamilakis 2014; Hamilakis et al. 2002; Hodder & Hutson 2003; Ingold & Vergunst 2016; Tilley 2008). People move at a range of spatial and temporal scales, regardless of whether a given society is thought to be residentially tethered to a particular location or to have a mobile lifestyle (Cribb 2004; Honeychurch & Makarewicz 2016; Murrieta-Flores 2009:249). Binford (1980) distinguished residential mobility, in which all members of a community move from one location to another, from logistical mobility, involving small groups moving to and from residential sites. People may engage in both of these and in other types of mobility, as is aptly demonstrated by archaeological evidence and ethnographic research, such as that indicating that for millennia herders moved between rich highland pastures in summer and the relative protection of lower elevations in winter (Frachetti 2011; see also Ingold & Vergunst's (2016) notion of 'ways of walking').

Several lines of evidence help track different types of human mobility across the landscape. Material traditions (conventions or 'styles' as expressed in artefacts) that people carry with them; the distributions of traded goods and raw materials from points of origin to destinations (e.g. as determined by physico-chemical signatures of source materials matched to 'final' destination goods); physical evidence of routes, paths and way markers etched across the landscape; and biological markers in human remains can all inform us on where people and things moved to and from (see Sections 2.2.1 and 2.3).

Movements occur at a range of scales and durations, from daily activities and routine journeys, seasonal rounds, pilgrimages and migrations. Navigating the landscape (or seascape) involves the recognition of physical elements that assist with decision-making, such as landmarks recognised from memory or other sources of information (Burke 2015). Mental maps or conceptual pathways composed of memories or stories can allow people to move decisively across the landscape without a necessity for formal, physical pathways: there can be routes without roads (see also Basso 1996; papers in Feld & Basso 1996).

Where seasonal routes have not left physical traces, movement across the landscape can be inferred from the seasonal use of occupation sites, revealed by the types of animal and plant remains left on, and now below, the ground. For example, the faunal and plant remains at the third millennium BCE (Late Neolithic) henge site of Durrington Walls in Wiltshire, England – part of the iconic landscape of Stonehenge (Pearson et al. 2020) – reveal far greater quantities of animal remains processed for food relative to plant foods (Craig et al. 2015). The faunal assemblage at this site is dominated by the remains of pigs, which were found in several midden deposits of food refuse and in pits. The remains of cattle are also present, along with those of other domesticates such as sheep and dog, and wild animals only occur occasionally. This is in keeping with other Late Neolithic assemblages of southern Britain. The density and treatment of the animal bones found in middens of food refuse outside houses at Durrington Walls suggest these are the remains of feasting (Albarella & Serjeanston 2002). Analysis of the pig bones and teeth indicate that pigs younger than one year old when killed had their bones deposited in these middens. The bones from older pigs aged between one and two years old were more often deposited in pits within the floors of houses, many during rituals of 'abandonment', associated with the 'closure' of individual houses (Wright et al. 2014:499, 510). The midden deposits have been interpreted as evidence of winter killings, while the pits indicate a preference for winter but a broader seasonal span compared with the middens (Wright et al. 2014:512). Such a conclusion could be reached because of the seasonal nature of pig births, so that the age of death could also be tracked to its corresponding season. The broader landscape of Stonehenge has long been associated with the midsummer solstice, but the preference for winter seasonal feasting events at Durrington Walls now reveals a ritualistic, social and subsistence celebratory landscape scheduled around both winter and summer events (Craig et al. 2015; Wright et al. 2014).

Routes that have been formalised by social habit or authority can also leave substantial material signatures that indicate the paths taken across the land. The travels of groups of people or herds of animals can produce visible paths trackable through compacted sediments, trodden vegetation with their distinctive disturbance-tolerant bordering vegetation taxa, micro-organisms and molluscs, curated surfaces or intentional depositions of material goods along the route (Gibson 2021; Ingold 2015). Some 'exceptional' travels may require the following of defined routes to reach a destination, with strategic points of visitation along the way. Such journeyings include pilgrimages, 'religiously motivated journeys to special places' (Skousen 2018:262). One of the best-known examples today is the *Camino de Santiago*, a network of pilgrims' routes active since the ninth century CE leading across western Europe to the cathedral of Santiago de Compostela, in Galicia in northwestern Spain. The convergence of people at particular places leaves traces in the landscape (see also Conkey 1980), and the establishment of defined routes connecting nodes of convergence (and, upon return, of dispersal), such as along the *Camino de Santiago*, ensure that the networks of movement between nodes result in the presence of identifiable structuring features in the archaeological landscape. These are also occasions for the coming together and dispersal of material goods, ideas and potentially newcomers back to the points of origin to which most pilgrims eventually return. In the case of the *Camino de Santiago*, for example, pilgrims have long carried scallop shells and objects marked with the symbol of the scallop. In medieval times, the pilgrims obtained the shells during visits to the Atlantic coast. They became a symbol of pilgrimage, announcing the pilgrim's state of religious communion in a culturally socialised landscape (Van Dyke 2018:4–5). Scallop shells, and representations of the shells made in other materials, continue to be an important part of the material culture found along the pilgrim network today.

The roads taken by the medieval pilgrims on the *Camino de Santiago* served multiple communities and purposes, and, usually, the pilgrims adopted already-established routes. The 'Winter Way', a seasonal route devised to bypass the winter snow in northern Spain, follows roads that had been constructed centuries earlier by the Romans. The vestiges of the Roman imperial road network highlight the multi-temporal nature of the landscape, and prompt us to think about the many social significations of roads and routes, relative to scale and durability. Formalised road networks have been seen as tools of empire, of all time periods (Witcher 1998:61). They serve as markers of order, prestige as well as pragmatism and invasion and are in themselves exclamations of landscape-scale cultural and politico-economic power (Horster & Hächler 2021). The Roman road network developed with the advance of Roman forces, but it was also used by civilians; it facilitated social interactions and commerce on many fronts, and it continued to do so for many years even after the fall of the Roman empire. Roman roads were new constructions in themselves, but there are convincing cases where they followed earlier routes, mapping onto Iron Age tracks in Britain, for example (Bishop 2014:2–15). The endurance of the roads long after the decline of Roman power presents a fascinating 'afterlife' of reuse, repurposing or disuse (Bishop 2014). Through the superimposition of Roman roads, earlier paths and later reuse, the road network emphasises landscapes as social products and media for social production and reproduction. In this sense, the Roman road networks also hold a lesson, and a warning, for archaeologists: there is a tendency for researchers to seek the origins or times of construction of archaeologically visible material expressions, such as those dating to when a road was first cobbled or a building first built. But we should not forget that a place continued to be engaged afterwards. A physical mark left from the original construction then affects future actions and perceptions of place, sometimes in very different ways to the original intent(s). A point often forgotten or conceptually erased away, the archaeology of such subsequent engagements is also of great interest to understanding the past, and eventually leads to the present.

2.2.1 Passing across the Waters

There is often bias in archaeology towards terrestrial contexts, reflected in the examples given thus far (and in the general use of the term 'landscape' to also refer to waterscapes). Waterways frequently provide physical and social barriers in the landscape, serving as impediments to movement or as territorial borders. Yet, navigable rivers, coastal routes and passages across the open ocean also provide appealing means of transport for goods and people. The places where land and water meet, at coasts and beside lakes and rivers, reveal the diverse ways in which people interact with waterscapes as well as landscapes. In regions of seasonal cold, discussion of waterscapes and landscapes ought also to consider a third, in-between and thus liminal state: snow and ice.

The First Nations peoples of northern and eastern Canada travelled the great rivers of this region by canoe in summer and by sled in winter, to hunt and trap, trade and socialise, moving between established settlements and seasonal campsites (Deal 2002; Stewart et al. 2004). Along the waterways, at locations where rapids or seasonal inundation made the waters unpassable, travellers created terrestrial paths to connect the navigable sections of the rivers. Known as 'portages' (or *louniguin* in the language of First Nations peoples living along the Saint John (Wolastoq) River: Nicholas Denys in Ganong 1899:119), canoes would be carried along these terrestrial trails to connect one waterway with another (Blair 2010; Ganong 1899:119; Moran 2020). Portages are material records of navigation, highlighting the ways that people negotiated the challenges of seasonal movement and created a dynamic landscape of terrestrial and riverine routes. Navigation of these routes was aided by way-marking the land, using temporary markers such as those recorded ethnographically (Gesner 1842; Mallery 1893) and more durable petroglyphs still evident in the landscape today. Historical birchbark maps (*wikhe'gan* in the language of the Peskotomuhkati) recording travel routes and journeys offer important records of past cultural knowledge, landscape perceptions, time and mobility (see Link 2, available as supplementary material at www.cambridge.org/mobilelandscapes). There are numerous documented records of such terrestrial and riverine-lacustrine networks in North America (e.g. the Grand Portage on Lake Superior), but those of eastern Canada are particularly rich in detail.

French explorer Samuel de Champlain's 1604 map of Saint John Harbour (Figure 1), in the province of New Brunswick, Canada, illustrates a portage skirting the formidable Reversing Falls. These rapids separate the lower Saint John River from the harbour and Bay of Fundy. Archaeological surveys and excavations revealed a substantial settlement site near one end of the portage, at Marble Cove on the Saint John River (Deal 2002:334; Fisher 1965; Sanger 1975:66). From Marble Cove, the route then climbed to the Douglas Avenue ridge, passing another extensive settlement site (the Bentley Street site) on the way down to the waters of the harbour (Suttie & Allen 2015). The Bentley Street site is located on an elevated bedrock shelf on what was clearly a significant route between the waters of the river and the harbour, thus part of a much more extensive route. The artefacts found at this site demonstrate that it was used most intensively during the Late and Transitional Archaic period (4,500–3,000 years ago), with its use extending back some 11,000 years to the Paleoindian period when the earliest migrants at the end of the Last Ice Age began moving into what is now Atlantic Canada (note that these cited ages have been estimated by the variably understood ages of the stone tool types present at the sites, not by the actual chronometric dating of the sites themselves). The site continued to be used into the period of contact with European explorers and colonists (Suttie 2003; Suttie & Allen 2015). Bentley Street remains a route from the harbour to the ridge in the present-day city of Saint John, a remarkable continuity in a much-changed landscape.

2.3 Methods

The physical record of paths and routes, and the sites and artefacts produced in relation to movement, can inform archaeologists about mobility across the landscape. The presence of artefacts that moved with people and animals can

Figure 1 Samuel de Champlain's 1604 map of Saint John Harbour, showing the portage to the east of Reversing Falls (top-left of image, annotated 'P') (from de Champlain 1613:30). From the collections of the New Brunswick Museum – Musée du Nouveau-Brunswick.

tell us where people spent time, where they travelled and where they sourced their possessions and technologies. The results of biomolecular, biochemical and physico-chemical analyses (Table 1) are used by archaeologists to reconstruct the diet and mobility of past peoples, illuminating human connections across space and through time, by identifying the resources that people used or the places where they spent time (e.g. see Link 3, available as supplementary material at www.cambridge.org/mobilelandscapes).

Table 1 Some recent genetic and physico-chemical techniques contributing to archaeological investigations of human connections across the landscape

Analysis	Technique	Evidence of mobility
Genetic	mtDNA, nuclear DNA, aDNA, eDNA	Population history; emergence of new alleles (variant forms of a gene)
Physico-chemical	Isotopic analyses: carbon ($\delta^{13}C$), nitrogen ($\delta^{15}N$), oxygen ($\delta^{18}O$), sulfur ($\delta^{34}S$), strontium ($^{87}Sr/^{86}Sr$), lead ($^{204, 206, 207, 208}Pb$) Elemental analyses: XRF	Regional differences in diet; past climate and environmental conditions; mobility via matching of individuals or populations with 'isoscapes' representing differences in available isotopic ranges Sourcing analyses; identification of activity areas

2.3.1 Isotopic Analyses

Archaeologists have been experimenting with isotopic analyses since the late 1970s to investigate past climates and environmental conditions, diet and mobility (e.g. Van der Merwe & Vogel 1978). Isotopic studies are based on ratios of stable to unstable isotopes of a given element in an archaeological sample, compared with its ratio in the environment. These isotopes may be stable and unchanging over time, or unstable and subject to degradation at known rates of decay. For example, carbon has three isotopes in nature: the two stable isotopes ^{12}C and ^{13}C, and the unstable (radioactive) isotope ^{14}C. The measurement of decay of ^{14}C (with its half-life of 5,730 ± 40 years) has well-known applications in archaeology in radiocarbon dating, while the ratio of stable carbon and nitrogen isotopes are widely used to determine an individual's or population's diet, each source food having its own chemical make-up and, with this, isotopic ratios. Isotopic analyses are particularly used to study the nature and frequency of marine versus terrestrial animal foods and the consumption of particular plant resources. Early work by Van der Merwe and Vogel (1978) applied such isotopic analyses to investigate diet from human bone collagen in skeletal remains, showing that maize was introduced to the Eastern Woodland region of North America around 1000 CE.

The measurement of isotopic ratios can be used to investigate habitat, diet and provenance because isotopes are present in the food and water that plants, animals and people consume. The isotopic ratios of elements present in rocks, soil, water, vegetation and animals vary by region. These elements are part of the local environment and, when plants, people and animals ingest food, water and medicines, the isotopic compounds in them enter the body and are incorporated into soft tissues, bone, tooth enamel, hair and nails (Frei & Price 2012:103–4). The isotopic signature of different parts of an individual's body can therefore be used to identify the geographical region from which their food and water sources came. For example, the geology of a region determines the amount of the stable isotopes strontium-87 (^{87}Sr) and strontium-86 (^{86}Sr) that are incorporated into the plants of that region, and therefore into the people and animals that consume those plants. When tooth enamel mineralises, its ^{87}Sr:^{86}Sr ratio from ingested materials enters the enamel as it forms. As the tooth grows, incremental layers capture the isotopic ratios produced from the foods it consumed through time, and with this the tooth becomes an isotopic archive of the region(s) that person or animal resided in or travelled through: a landscape biography as it were. Teeth grow from top to bottom, producing time sequences and isotopic records. Changes in isotopic ratios can be linked with movement from one place to another, while consistent isotopic ratios suggest that a person remained in the same area, although regions with roughly the same isotopic signatures can be extensive. The ability to map where an individual spent time is only as precise as the available knowledge of comparative regional environmental isotopic ratios – the 'baseline' data – yet provides a fascinating way to investigate mobility (or degrees of sedentariness) in a person's lifetime.

The differences in formation rates of tooth enamel, bone, hair and nails result in records that represent different phases of an individual's life. Human tooth enamel forms during early childhood and is normally complete by age six, with the exception of wisdom teeth that take longer to form (Price 2014:72). The biochemical signature of most tooth enamel therefore reflects the nutrients eaten by the child, and often the child's mother, in their early years. Bone, on the other hand, is a more dynamic material; the structural protein in bone, collagen, regularly changes and is replaced over time. The biochemical signal from bone therefore reflects the diet and landscape in which an individual lived during the years immediately before their death. Rapidly growing keratinous tissues, such as hair and nails, likewise change over time, with old material replaced by new, preserving regional isotopic values in time sequence (Hu et al. 2020). These components of an individual's body can therefore be used to reconstruct their travel history in the later years of their life. Together, these bioarchaeological components and their isotopic analyses allow archaeologists to examine aspects of the life history of individuals and to comment on their mobility across the landscape and connections to places.

These analyses are not limited to people. Oxygen or strontium isotope analyses of animal hair, fur or fleece can provide information about where an animal or a person lived based on internal dietary indicators and also on external environ-mental factors, from the water that the hair or fleece was exposed to (Hu et al. 2020; Tipple et al. 2018). This provides information about the animal's life history and also about the regions from which people sourced materials such as wool.

Isotopic analyses of human or animal remains to discuss mobility or connec-tions to particular environments also require knowledge about the distribution of isotopic ratios across the land. The development of such baseline databases has resulted in 'isoscapes', maps representing the distribution of environmental isotopic ratio signatures and showing the spatial variations of the isotopic material(s) of interest (Bowen 2010). Isoscapes have been produced for a number of elements, and the analytical method can be applied globally in archaeology, ecology, forensic science, geology and other fields (Figure 2).

These relatively new methods are allowing archaeologists to map the mobil-ity of individuals and to identify the places in which they spent their lives, in far greater detail than previously possible. The 'Egtved Girl' (or 'Egtved Woman') is a Bronze Age young woman whose well-preserved burial near Egtved in Denmark was first excavated in 1921. The woman's oak coffin has been dated

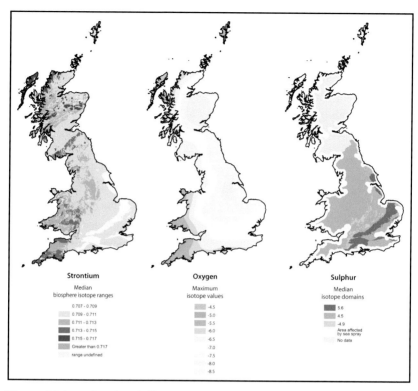

Figure 2 Maps showing differences in isotopic values recorded across Britain. The range of median $^{87}Sr/^{86}Sr$ values are from water, vegetation, bone and dentine samples. The maximum oxygen isotope values are from groundwater samples ($\delta^{18}O$ ‰ (VSMOW)). The median sulphur isotope values ($\delta^{34}S$ (VCDT)) are from vegetation samples (after British Geological Survey materials © UKRI (2020); see also Evans et al. 2018).

by dendrochronology to 1370 BCE (Kristiansen & Larsson 2005). The water-logged, acidic conditions of the burial mound, followed by careful conservation, preserved the ox hide on which her body was placed, the woven blanket covering her body, the corded skirt and woollen blouse she wore, her hair, nails and tooth enamel. A vessel made of bark and a small bundle contained cremated skeletal remains of a five- to six-year-old child (Frei et al. 2015). Strontium isotope analyses of the Egtved Girl, the child, textiles and animal hide are now revealing new dimensions of Bronze Age mobility. Isotopic analysis of the tooth enamel, compared with strontium isoscapes from Denmark and adjacent areas, indicate that the sixteen- to eighteen-year-old girl did not grow up in the area where she was buried. Her shoulder-length hair provided information about where she had been over a period of twenty-three months before her death

(Frei et al. 2015:4). The oldest and most recent segments of her hair revealed high strontium isotope signatures, while the middle sections reflected a lower signature, characteristic of Denmark (Frei & Price 2012:110). Her nails and the wool used to produce her clothing returned results similar to her most recent hair, reinforcing the interpretation that she had been outside Denmark shortly before her death. Strontium isotope analyses of the child returned results that match the values obtained from the Egtved Girl's tooth enamel, suggesting that this child had grown up in the same region as the girl. The ages of the two individuals make it unlikely that this is a mother and child, but the two appear to have spent their early years in the same location.

By comparing the strontium isotope signatures found in the child's bones, the girl's tooth enamel and parts of her hair, the researchers concluded that these two individuals could have grown up in several regions, including Sweden, Britain and large parts of south and central Europe. Objects from southwestern Germany found with the girl suggest that this might be the most likely region (Frei et al. 2015:5), although the possession of cultural objects does not necessarily equate to a person's origin, in part because objects could have been traded in or otherwise obtained. The case of the Egtved Girl emphasises that isotopic analyses do not always provide precise itineraries, but the technique reveals that this young woman had travelled hundreds of kilometres in her short life. She had also travelled back and forth, coming to Denmark from her place of birth, leaving again and then returning very shortly before her death. The person and the possessions of the Egtved Girl reveal her connections with multiple places within a wide range. They provide new evidence for networks of mobility within Bronze Age Europe that can be further investigated by the transportation of objects.

The 'Skrydstrup Woman' presents a similar burial, also in Denmark and dated to 1300–1100 BCE on the basis of associated artefact types and a radiocarbon sample taken from the woman's scalp hair (Frei et al. 2017). This burial mound and oak coffin of a seventeen- to eighteen-year-old female was excavated in 1935 in southern Denmark (Frei et al. 2017). In common with the Egtved Girl and other oak coffin burials, the coffin was lined with an ox hide and the woman wore woollen clothing. Strontium isotope analyses performed on tooth enamel indicate that this individual had not grown up in the area where she was buried. The range of strontium values returned from the woman's long hair indicates that between forty-two and forty-seven months prior to her death she had travelled (recording a large range of strontium values) from her birthplace to the area of southern Denmark and had remained in that area for the rest of her life (Frei et al. 2017:13). Despite these similar histories, the strontium isotope signatures of the first molars of the Egtved Girl and the Skrydstrup Woman indicate different areas of origin for these two individuals (Frei et al. 2017:16).

The location of these two burials is also interesting within the broader social landscape in which these women lived; the burials are part of a larger regional network of monumental mounds (Felding 2016:14–5; Holst & Rasmussen 2013). The mounds are positioned at a geographic and geological division between flat and sandy land to the west and glacial moraines and hills to the east. A Bronze Age trade route running through what is now Denmark followed this geographic division (Kristiansen & Suchowska-Ducke 2015), meaning that the burials are near established supra-regional routes of Bronze Age Scandinavia.

The burials also prompt us to reflect on the role of time and our interpretation of it from the archaeological record. The burials of the Egtved Girl and Skrydstrup Woman could each be interpreted as a single event, and yet the archaeological items they are associated with, including the remains of the individuals, inform us about a *span* of time and activities within that time frame. The oak coffin burials are more generally part of a long tradition of burial mound construction in southern Scandinavia, extending from 1700 to 1000 BCE (Holst et al. 2001). The burials of the two women therefore represent momentary *events*, yet inform on mobilities over human lifespans, and project enduring messages about cultural connections to a particular place expressed through a shared tradition of human modification of landscape by the construction of prominent burial mounds.

The results of the isotopic analyses on the Egtved Girl and Skrydstrup Woman have been questioned by some researchers on the basis that the reference data used to create the strontium isoscape, which is in turn used to determine which samples are considered local or non-local, may have been contaminated by modern agricultural lime (Thomsen & Andreasen 2019; Thomsen et al. 2021). The researchers nevertheless stand by their analyses (Frei et al. 2022), again on the basis of sample location selections for baseline data, emphasising the complexities of defining representative isoscapes and in developing multi-proxy baselines (Ladergaard-Pedersen et al. 2021). This debate highlights the need for the careful selection of samples to ensure reliability, and multi-proxy investigations where possible, to minimise the limitations of each method and thereby strengthen the overall results and interpretations. It also emphasises the point that *the details matter*, a principle that runs through all the sections of this volume.

2.3.2 Multiple Methods

We find an example of the use of multiple methods by returning to our earlier case of Durrington Walls in Britain, where there was evidence of winter feasting on pigs suggesting the seasonal nature of activity types. Isotopic analyses investigating where the animals enjoyed at the feasts came from are now providing further insights into the role of the Durrington Walls in the broader social landscape. Analyses of five isotope ratios ($^{87}Sr:^{86}Sr$, $^{34}S:^{32}S$, $^{18}O:^{16}O$, $^{13}C:^{12}C$ and $^{15}N:^{14}N$) conducted on the remains of 131 pigs from four Late Neolithic henge complexes, including 89 pigs from Durrington Walls, have revealed that few of the pigs were raised locally (Madgwick et al. 2019). The pigs from Durrington Walls have a larger range of isotopes than those from any of the other comparative Late Neolithic sites, all of which are located on the relatively well-understood chalk lithologies of Wessex (for examples of these isoscapes, see Figure 2). Pigs are not seasonally mobile, nor are they well-suited to long-distance travel. As the principal domesticate of Neolithic Britain, they might also be assumed to have generally been sourced locally. The fact that these animals were not local provides a reasonable proxy for human movements, given that the animals' travels would have been accompanied by people.

These results can be paired with work on the origins of forty-nine cattle also found at Durrington Walls (Evans et al. 2019), second only to pigs in the faunal record. They, too, indicate local and distant origins. The material culture from the Late Neolithic (2800–2400 BCE) does not include artefacts from the European continent, so the origins of the non-local pigs and cattle were considered in the context of the British Isles (Evans et al. 2019:5195; Madgwick et al. 2019). The diverse origins of some cattle and many pigs brought by people to Durrington Walls, including from locations in what is now Scotland and Wales, indicate that this site was a significant node in an extensive social network, and an important place in regional perceptions of connectivity.

2.3.3 Ancient DNA

Long-term views of human population locationality and movement across the landscape are possible by identifying and tracing similarities and differences in DNA signatures of organisms across place and through time (see Link 4, available as supplementary material at www.cambridge.org/mobilelandscapes). The analysis of genetic markers includes extraction of ancient DNA (aDNA) – mitochondrial DNA (mtDNA), passed down through the biological mother; Y-chromosomes (Y-DNA), from the biological father; or autosomal (often better known as 'nuclear') DNA, from the biological mother and father combined – and the sequencing of ancient genomes. A genome refers to a complete set of all an organism's DNA passed from one generation to the next via reproduction. Early research in aDNA began in the mid-1980s (Higuchi et al. 1984; Pääbo 1985), with the first complete sequence of an ancient human genome generated in 2010 (Rasmussen et al. 2010).

Each 'data point' in human DNA analysis represents an individual person. A DNA strand is made up of four nucleotide bases: adenine (A), thymine (T), guanine (G) and cytosine (C). These bases pair specifically on opposite strands, such that a C always pairs with a G and an A always with a T, and the pattern formed by these pairs encodes the information specific to that part of the DNA molecule. In nuclear DNA, located in the nucleus of every cell, a single, full set of forty-six chromosomes containing genetic material from maternal and paternal ancestors (diploid) undergo recombination ('shuffling' of both parents' DNA) and is therefore altered through reproduction. Mitochondrial DNA, on the other hand, exists in hundreds of tiny cell components (mitochondria) outside the nucleus of each cell, but consists of only one chromosome. Mitochondrial DNA is inherited from the maternal line only (haploid) and does not undergo genetic recombination, meaning that any variation in mtDNA is due to genetic mutation. Nuclear DNA contains more information than mtDNA, but the stability of mtDNA and the hundreds of copies of it in each cell mean that it is more easily retrieved from archaeological materials. Both types of DNA can be sequenced, as can Y-chromosomes that come from the father only.

The first human genome was sequenced just over a decade ago, and ever since there has been a florescence of genetic studies. As new techniques developed, important debates emerged over the role of aDNA analyses in studies of human communities, mobility and multi-generational connections to places (Furholt 2018; Sykes et al. 2019). Genetics researchers often ask questions about the human past that are different to those asked by archaeologists, and often see advantages in maintaining relatively simplistic models so that they can be reliably tested with the available data (Sykes et al. 2019:504). But the master narratives that are often paired with these models, of sweeping migrations and population replacements, largely replicate early twentieth-century culture-historical explanatory models, and in archaeology they trigger disciplinary anxieties about repeating past mistakes. The culture-historical archaeologies of the early twentieth century sought to define the regions from which archaeo-logical assemblages were found, and to associate particular lands with named cultural groups, such as the 'Beaker People' or 'Corded Ware culture' (now called the 'Bell Beaker Complex' and 'Corded Ware Complex', respectively). For some (e.g. Kossinna 1911), archaeological cultures were equated with present-day ethnic groups and considered to share the same biological or genetic classification as well as cultural heritage (think of the deeply problem-atic self-designation of the 'Aryan'). Together, with the search for origins that underlies culture-historical approaches, this resulted in social-evolutionary narratives that conflated ideas about national identity with biological ancestry and connected these ideas with the archaeological record to make irredentist claims to territory (Eisenmann et al. 2018; Heyd 2017). Extensive research across the humanities and social sciences on the concepts of identity, ethnicity, kinship and culture has emphasised the impossibility of equating genetic make-up, with which one is born, with ethnic or cultural identities, which one learns. It would be hypocritical for archaeologists not to learn from their disciplinary past; given the historical entanglement of these issues, there is a need to proceed with extra caution when it comes to the interpretative scope of studies of genetic heritage and population movements.

The majority of scientists publishing genetic studies are quite aware of the difference between genetic groupings and archaeological assemblages. Yet, successive calls have been made for more careful use of terminologies that might casually conflate 'cultural' groupings of people who share material practices with sets of people who are genetically similar, primarily to avoid confusion among non-specialists, including the media and politicians (Eisenmann et al. 2018; Frieman & Hoffmann 2019; Haak et al. 2015; Hakenbeck 2019; Heyd 2017). Parsing complex ideas and analyses into comprehensible findings that retain precision but avoid overly simplistic explanations is a critical challenge for the field of archaeogenetics (palaeogenetics, palaeogenomics). To avoid the offenses of the past and to constructively contribute to archaeological debates, the precision achieved in communicating results needs to match the scientific precision demanded in the methodologies of this developing field.

With these cautions and aspirations in mind, aDNA has the capacity to make important contributions to the study of human mobility. Paired with archaeological evidence, it has the potential to help better understand the activities and movements of people in the past, as they traversed their landscapes through lifetimes and across generations. A constructive friction but exciting potential exists in the archaeological responses to the growing number of aDNA studies. The genome-wide analyses of aDNA are proving to be transformative for the study of individuals and populations over time, but successful and meaningful results rely on the collection of genome-wide information from adequate numbers of individuals by which to extrapolate from the individual to the population (Haak et al. 2015:207).

At present, the majority of genome-wide data come from western Eurasia (Eisenmann et al. 2018:2). They have been used to investigate the macro-scale movements of people in the Chalcolithic, Neolithic and Early Bronze Ages (c. 8000–3000 BCE). These studies have accounted for modern European genetic groupings by positing several major migrations, the first being an Early Neolithic migration of agriculturalists from the ancient Near East westward into Europe (Mathieson et al. 2015). In the early third millennium (c. 2900 BCE), a dramatic increase in a new genomic component occurred in north-central Europe and southern Scandinavia: pastoralist communities that lived on the Pontic-Caspian Steppe are the best-known proxy for this genetic component (Kristiansen et al. 2017). This genetic component later (c. 2400–2000 BCE) spread from the European continent to the British Isles. These aDNA results themselves are not at issue; individual studies might be critiqued on the basis of sample size or methodology, but the overall results have been replicated in multiple studies. Rather, the problem lies in the abstract and simplified relationships that have been asserted between this genetic record of movements and the archaeological knowledge of the diversity of individual and collective production of culture, use of landscape and connections to place. Rather than offering archaeology a way to 'escape' theoretical debates or 'solve' big questions, as suggested by Kristiansen (2014), aDNA results instead demand debate and offer opportunities for archaeologists to refine their 'master narratives' (Crellin & Harris 2020).

In a return to questions of timing and scale, both of evidence and of interpretation, archaeologists have developed finer-grained studies to assess whether aDNA can assist in explaining more localised regional patterns of transformation, which the broader-scale narratives do not adequately explain. Ken Massy and colleagues responded to supra-regional studies with a 'micro-historical' study investigating the mobility of Late Neolithic and Early Bronze Age communities in the Lech Valley, Germany (Massy et al. 2017). The evidence from burials in this region indicates that there were local continuities of practice during the later third and early second millennia BCE (Massy et al. 2017:242). Using DNA samples extracted from the teeth of eighty-seven individuals, radiocarbon dated to a range between 2500 and 1700 cal BCE, the researchers obtained genome-wide data for sixty of these individuals (Massy et al. 2017; Stockhammer et al. 2015). Isotopic analyses (C, N, O, Sr) provided additional information on the diet and mobility of each individual (Massy et al. 2017:246). The combination of isotopic and mtDNA results indicates a population that 'combined individual long-distance mobility (already, or at least, or especially during childhood) with continuous settlement in the Lech Valley' (Massy et al. 2017:256). Investigating the same time period of 2500–1700 cal BCE (Late Neolithic to Early Bronze Age) in the Lech Valley, Knipper et al. (2017) examined mtDNA haplotype matches and strontium isotope ratios, finding matrilocal relationships between local groups (where a male partner goes to live with the female's community) but patrilocal negotiations (in which the female partner goes to live in the male's community) with distant groups during the Neolithic to Early Bronze Age. Thus, transdisciplinary approaches, in which aDNA is investigated alongside isotopic analyses and in which studies of culture and kinship inform the results, are providing new insights about mobility, social associations and connections to place.

A final case study highlights a new development in the ability to determine past connections between people and places through archaeology and genetic research. DNA has previously been extracted from the bones of Neanderthals, meaning that Neanderthal genomic sequences can now be recognised (Mafessoni et al. 2020). In 2017, researchers showed that mtDNA could be extracted not just from human skeletal remains or other parts of the body but also from the Pleistocene sediments along which hominins walked (environmental aDNA (eDNA) coming from terrestrial sediments, often abbreviated as sedaDNA) (Slon et al. 2017). Even more recently, researchers revealed that Neanderthal nuclear aDNA can also be thus recovered (Vernot et al. 2021). From carefully collected and processed samples of Pleistocene cave sediments from Europe and Eurasia (Galería de les Estatuas in northern Spain; Chagyrskaya and Denisova Caves in the Altai mountains of Russia), Neanderthal DNA was identified from layers dated to between 200,000 and 50,000 years old (Vernot et al. 2021). One group of Neanderthals was identified as living in the Galería de les Estatuas around 130,000 years ago. A second, more genetically modern group was identified as inhabiting the same cave around 100,000 years ago.

The significance of this for landscape archaeology and for the study of ancient hominin and human population movements is extraordinary. Bones and teeth certainly still offer more detailed genomic information, from which richer and more complex discussions of past human movements across the landscape can be developed. But there is now the possibility to use the sedimentary record, in stratified and chronologically controlled deposits, to investigate who lived at a place, who they were genetically related to and the degree to which such associations may have genetically changed over time. Genetic change is a certainty, as nuclear DNA is recombined, so it is not a question of seeking an 'original' population but of beginning to articulate the complex socio-spatial relationships of ancient communities within sites and across the landscape (genetic 'landscape histories'). When discussing genetic ancestry, we often use the analogy of a tree, with branches dividing into increasingly discrete genetic stems and shoots. But in a landscape analogy often used by palaeoanthropologists, our early genetic history is best considered like a braided stream, in which channels diverge only to converge again downstream, a result of complex histories of social connections and genetic re-combinations.

The evidence from aDNA studies engages with concepts of origins, migrations and population replacements, highlighting shared genetic heritages as much as identifying their differences. Groups with shared biological ancestry are certainly able to be classified, with these genetic classifications contributing to narratives of broad-scale population shifts over many generations, such as in the multiple migrations of early modern humans into the Middle East, Asia and

Europe, or the movements of early Neolithic farming communities from Western Asia into Europe. Yet in themselves, geographical and temporal patterns in the DNA results enable archaeologists and geneticists to sharpen the focus of their *questions*, rather than providing *explanations*. Once again, the issue of spatial and temporal scales and their resolution across the landscape is front and centre. The macro-scale of grand narratives such as long-term trends in human mobility – the epic journeys of humanity's distant ancestors – are being balanced by more localised studies that investigate smaller landscapes in greater detail, to achieve more nuanced understandings and narratives of local mobility, kinship and connections to place. 'Big history' is not necessarily about global or widespread movements and relations. For some people, the biggest and most important history is the most local; it is about the local landscape with which people are affiliated and that render places enduring and *persistent*. Again, transdisciplinary studies prove most effective in this regard.

2.4 Further Readings

Aldred, O. (2020). *The Archaeology of Movement*. Milton: Taylor & Francis Group.

Basso, K. (1996).*Wisdom Sits in Places: Landscape and Language Among the Western Apache*. Albuquerque: University of New Mexico Press.

Binford, L. R. (1982). The archaeology of place. *Journal of Anthropological Archaeology* 1(1):5–31. https://doi.org/10.1016/0278-4165(82)90006-X.

Crellin, R. J. & Harris, O. J. (2020). Beyond binaries: Interrogating ancient DNA. *Archaeological Dialogues* 27(1):37–56. https://doi.org/10.1017/S1380203820 000082.

Evans, J., Pearson, M. P., Madgwick, R., Sloane, H. & Albarella, U. (2019). Strontium and oxygen isotope evidence for the origin and movement of cattle at Late Neolithic Durrington Walls, UK. *Archaeological and Anthropological Sciences* 11(10):5181–97. https://doi.org/10.1007/s12520-019-00849-w.

Feld, S. & Basso, K. H. (Eds.) (1996). *Senses of Place*. Santa Fe: School for Advanced Research.

Frei, K. M., Mannering, U., Kristiansen, K., et al. (2015). Tracing the dynamic life story of a Bronze Age female. *Scientific Reports* 5(1):1–7. https://doi.org/ 10.1038/srep10431

Ingold, T. (1993). The temporality of landscape. *World Archaeology* 25(2): 152–74. https://doi.org/10.1080/00438243.1993.9980235.

Haak, W., Lazaridis, I., Patterson, N., et al. (2015). Massive migration from the steppe was a source for Indo-European languages in Europe. *Nature* 522 (7555):207–11. https://doi.org/10.1038/nature14317.

Lucas, G. (2021). *The Archaeology of Time Revisited*. London: Routledge.

Madgwick, R., Lamb, A. L., Sloane, H., et al. (2019). Multi-isotope analysis reveals that feasts in the Stonehenge environs and across Wessex drew people and animals from throughout Britain. *Science Advances* 5(3):eaau6078. https://doi.org/10.1126/sciadv.aau6078.

Schiffer, M. B. (1985). Is there a 'Pompeii Premise' in archaeology? *Journal of Anthropological Research* 41(1):18–41. https://doi.org/10.1086/jar.41.1 .3630269.

Vernot, B., Zavala, E. I., Gómez-Olivencia, A., et al. (2021). Unearthing Neanderthal population history using nuclear and mitochondrial DNA from cave sediments. *Science* 372(6542):p.eabf1667. www.science.org/doi/ 10.1126/science.abf1667.

3 The Physical Landscapes of Past Societies

Understanding where people went and when, what they did where and how they interacted on the ground requires understanding the geographical contexts of people's lives. This requires positioning individual sites and their archaeological records in their past environmental settings. These palaeoenvironments were rarely what they are today, especially those of the deeper past. Topographic features such as slopes, rock outcrops, ridge tops, coastlines and hydrographic networks have all changed through time (see Link 5, available as supplementary material at www.cambridge.org/mobilelandscapes), as have climate regimes and vegetation and faunal communities (see Link 6, available as supplementary material at www.cambridge.org/mobilelandscapes), so the scope for environmental reconstruction is rather large. Along with these changes in the physical layout of the landscape, the distribution of targeted habitats and resources, the accessibility of certain locations and the routes and travel strategies by which people connected with others and accessed places and resources will often also have changed. It can be difficult to truly gauge what places may have looked like (and what of the senses other than sight?), how their fine details influenced past human actions and the opportunities and constraints they may have afforded in the past. How, then, can archaeologists reconstruct those past physical settings, and what kinds of things should they consider when defining a research approach to address past social landscapes?

3.1 Thinking About the Physical Settings of Archaeological Sites

As evident from all the issues and examples discussed in Section 2, it is important to think of archaeological sites not just as isolated locations but also as situated in broader landscapes (e.g. Lacroix et al. 2014). Here we address three dimensions of past landscapes through one case study each:

1. Changes to a site's surrounding environment.
2. How archaeological sites may be conceptually 'anchored' to their surroundings.
3. The physical accessibility of archaeological sites.

We focus on caves because of their enduring locations as sheltered places, repeatedly attracting occupation often over many thousands of years. Caves also have another advantage over many other types of archaeological sites: as well-sheltered underground environments, they typically offer good protection from the elements, and are thus conducive to unusually high levels of preservation of the cultural materials and installations they house. Caves therefore serve as enduring places that present distinctive intra-site landscapes and offer well-preserved records that can inform us of the broader landscapes in which they formed.

3.1.1 Changes to a Site's Surrounding Environment: Cosquer Cave

Cosquer cave is a clear example of a site whose human use, in this case during the Upper Palaeolithic, took place in a completely different environmental setting to that of today. Today the cave's entrance lies 37 m below the Mediterranean Sea, at the foot of the Calanques limestone massif just to the northeast of the Riou Archipelago near Marseille in France (Bard & Lambeck 2000; Clottes et al. 1992, 2005; Figures 3 and 4). It is, therefore, only accessible

Figure 3 Profiles of the Calanques massif rising above the Mediterranean Sea. The entrance to Cosquer Cave is found 37 m below the current sea level (photos by Bruno Arfib).

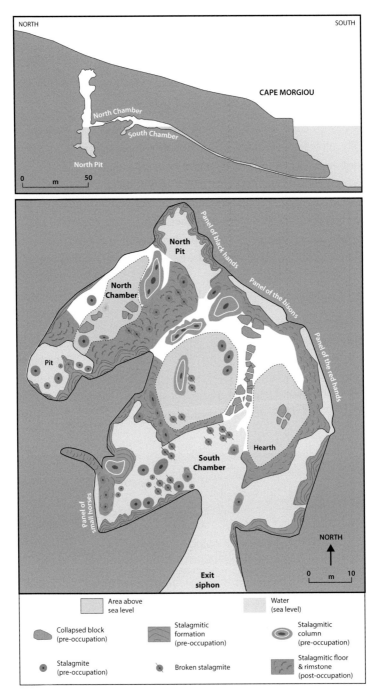

Figure 4 Cosquer Cave. Top: Cross section through the cave and its entrance passage. Bottom: Plan of the cave (after Collina-Girard & Arfib 2010: figure 4).

by diving, at a depth requiring specialised scuba-diving equipment beyond the means of Upper Palaeolithic peoples. A 175 m-long submerged passage through the rock leads to an open cave chamber above the surface of the sea, where 505 rock art depictions can still be seen today (Valladas et al. 2017). Radiocarbon ages on some of the charcoal paintings reveal two main phases of painting activity: the first c. 33,000–30,000 cal BP, and the second c. 25,000–21,000 cal BP, with paintings and stencils also having been made during the intermediate period (Valladas et al. 2017:632). Some of the submerged walls are engraved (any pigment art below the water level would have long been washed away by the seawater), and while it can be reasonably presumed that they date to one of these phases, they remain undated. In common with other rock art sites of southern France, the cave contains the usual European Upper Palaeolithic rock art bestiary such as horse, ibex, aurochs, bison and deer, supplemented by rarer marine fauna such as seal and Great Auk or penguin (e.g. Clottes et al. 2005; d'Errico 1994). Both the main rock art phases at Cosquer Cave – and thus both the main phases of human occupation – date to the Last Glacial Maximum (Marine Isotope Stage (MIS) 2), the peak of the Last Ice Age. This was a period when global sea levels were c. 120 m lower than they are today. But where, precisely, was the Mediterranean Sea's water level at the time the rock art was made and the site occupied? This question is important because it would enable us to understand Cosquer Cave's position relative to resource zones, the coastal and hinterland landscapes of human habitation and the environmental contexts of mobility patterns; that is, the endurance of the site in its broader land-and-seascape (for notions of persistent places in contexts of environmental change, see e.g. Maher 2019; Schlanger 1992; Shaw et al. 2016).

The current proximity of the sea creates a false impression of a coastal setting for Cosquer Cave's Upper Palaeolithic occupation and for its human population. Yet reconstruction of the cave's palaeoenvironment gives a very different reading (Collina-Girard 2014). At the time of its occupation, a vast continental shelf was exposed on either side of the cave (Figure 5). Today three separate palaeoshorelines can be identified, at around –50, –90 and –100 m below current sea level (Collina-Girard 2014). In addition to these palaeoshorelines, a steep downturn in slope around –130 to –135 m marks the upper rims of two deep submarine canyons, the Planier and Cassidaigne canyons, respectively. They are part of an older phase of the geological history of the Mediterranean, at such depths that they were never exposed as dry land when Cosquer Cave was occupied. Rather, the rims of the two canyons formed part of the coastline during the Last Glacial Maximum (Cita 1982; Clauzon et al. 1996). The dating of relic biota associated with these ancient coasts, such as marine shells, reveals that sea levels in the immediate vicinity of the cave were –135 m lower than present during the Last Glacial Maximum, –100 m around

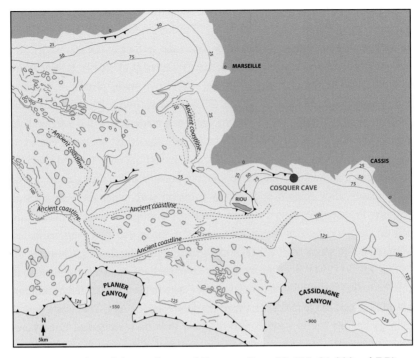

Figure 5 Plan of the environs of Cosquer Cave 33,000–21,000 cal BP)
(after Collina-Girard 1996: figure 4).

14,000 BP (= c. 17,000 cal BP), and –80 m around 11,700 BP (= c. 13,500 cal BP)
(Collina-Girard 1996:38–39). The entrance to Cosquer Cave became submerged
sometime between 9,000 and 7,000 cal BP (Antonioli 2012; Arfib 2021; Collina-
Girard 1996:35; Lichter et al. 2010).

Drawing together the geomorphological evidence, Cosquer Cave's landforms can be reconstructed for the period of the cave's occupation. The cave
was situated at the foot of a limestone escarpment. The entrance faced out onto
a vast, rugged limestone plateau riddled with karst depressions, with river
valleys and canyons up to several hundred metres deep, such as in the current
Riou Archipelago. The sea was located just over 5 km to the southwest, but the
vistas from the cave's entrance were entirely terrestrial (Figures 5 and 6). This
rugged landscape was covered with a steppe vegetation that supported the fauna
depicted in the cave's rock art. Further away, maritime habitats probably also
influenced why the cave was chosen for occupation: positioned at an ecotone
between mountain, plateau and sea, it held a strategic geographical position near
the intersection of major land systems. Access to the cave's two large chambers
was entirely through dry land via the now-submerged entrance passage that
would then have, as today, lain pitch-dark 180 m into the rock (Figure 4).

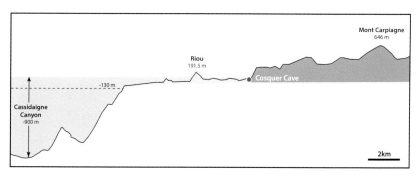

Figure 6 Cross section through the Cosquer Cave landscape indicating sea levels 33,000–21,000 cal BP (dotted line) and today (after Coloco 2019[1]).

Cosquer Cave was richly endowed with speleothems during the Last Glacial Maximum, when people created its archaeological deposits, as evidenced by the many paintings on its columns and other rock formations (Figure 7) (Olive & Vanrell 2021). Inside the cave, stalagmites and columns divide the cave into two smaller chambers, with the innermost chamber terminating at a large pit. The pit signals a major obstacle inside the cave; its edge is marked by a set of hand stencils. This marking of the underground landscape at critical points along passageways is common also in other Spanish and French Upper Palaeolithic caves with analogous topographic features (e.g. Cueva de la Garma, Cueva de la Pileta; Arias & Ontañon 2012, 2014; Simón Vallejo et al. 2021; Vanrell & Olive 2021b). However, the cave has not always been like this, and determining what was there at the time of its occupation versus what there is today requires geomorphological study. A detailed mapping enables fragments of speleothems broken by people and now lying on the floor to be matched to their original parent speleothems through their remnant stumps, showing that when people were in the cave they broke speleothems, modifying how the cave chambers could be travelled through, and the activities that took place.

The example of Cosquer Cave shows how the cave's configuration and its surrounding environment have changed through time. While it could be said that some aspects, such as past sea levels, are already broadly understood, the specific details and exact geomorphological setting required considerable research to precisely understand the changes that have taken place. A nuanced understanding requires detailed study, careful mapping and informed visual representation to allow both researchers and the public alike to truly visualise

---

[1] www.coloco.org/projets/calanques/.

Figure 7 Three painted horses preserved above the waterline in Cosquer Cave (photo by Luc Vanrell).

what the cave and its surrounds were like at the time of its occupation, and to thus better understand how people traversed and occupied the place in the past. We describe in more detail the methods of such mapping in Section 4.

3.1.2 How Archaeological Sites May Be Conceptually 'Anchored' to Their Surroundings: Chauvet Cave

In contrast to Cosquer Cave, Chauvet Cave is far removed from the Mediterranean and its oscillating sea levels and shifting coastlines. At first glance, the deeply incised gorges and geologically ancient limestone massifs of the Ardèche River in southeastern France signal long-standing landforms. But this impression can lead to the false assumption that the current landscape is much like it was during the Upper Palaeolithic, when people frequented the cave and produced its many paintings within the calibrated age ranges of c. 34,500–37,500 cal BP and again c. 30,000–31,500 cal BP (Clottes 1996; Quiles et al. 2016) (Figure 8). However, charcoal torch marks on the cave walls also date to intervening times, as well as to a few millennia after the second phase of painting, signalling that people returned to the cave in-between the two major phases and afterwards.

Today's Chauvet Cave environment is geologically deeply incised and dramatic, combining the entrances of gorges, an imposing natural archway

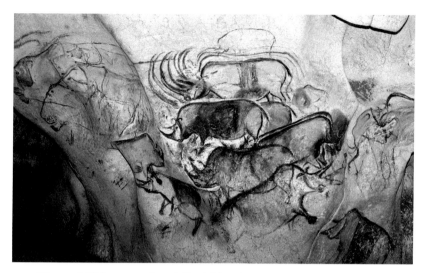

Figure 8 Rhinoceros Panel, End Chamber, Chauvet Cave (photo by Carole Fritz).

(the Pont d'Arc) through which flows the Ardèche River, and a broad abandoned river meander (the Combe d'Arc) – now a low, sediment-filled terrace – from which rises a rocky escarpment housing the cave's entrance (Figure 9). But which of these landforms already existed at the time of the cave's occupation going back some 34,500–37,500 cal BP, and which have formed since? Had the archway over the river already formed? Did the river then run through the now-abandoned Combe d'Arc meander? Was the topography of the cliff-lined amphitheatre in which the cave is found morphologically akin to the landform that can be seen today? These questions are important for understanding the configuration of the land at the time of Chauvet Cave's occupation, giving context to the site's engagements, and indeed to that of the occupation of all twenty-three known Upper Palaeolithic sites in the gorges of the Ardèche River, of which Chauvet Cave is by far the most decorated with rock art.

Perhaps the most obvious question to ask concerns the cave's entrance. Today, Chauvet Cave is entered through a small and narrow hole at ground level. Without knowing in advance its exact location, one would be unlikely to find it unless walking past it, as it cannot be seen from any great distance. But this was not the entrance at the time of the cave's occupation. Detailed geomorphological mapping of the cave coupled with three-dimensional laser scanning enabled its massive palaeo-entryway and entrance passage to be reconstructed in 3D, revealing that Chauvet Cave was once easily seen from a long way away: its domed entrance was an impressive 20 m wide and 8 m high (Delannoy et al. 2010).

Figure 9 Chauvet Cave in its current physical setting. (A) Panoramic view of the Combe d'Arc meander and the Cirque d'Estre cliff-line in which opens the entrance to Chauvet Cave. (B) Major physical features of the Chauvet Cave landscape. (C) and (D) The natural pathway that gradually climbs from the base of the limestone cliff at the edge of the ancient Combe d'Arc meander to the entrance of Chauvet Cave (photos and artwork by Jean-Jacques Delannoy).

This Pleistocene entryway was identified from the accumulated rockfall that today seals the inner side of the palaeo-entrance. The cave would have been visible from the valley floor and must have drawn attention, especially as a long, linear incision ran along the base of the cliff straight to the cave. This incised cliff-line demarcates a limestone ledge that connected the bottom of the valley to the limestone plateau via the cave. The ledge remains a prominent feature of the cliff today, except that the old cave entrance is no longer visible (Figures 9 and 10). This natural path was the one taken by the animals and people who frequented the cave, just as it is the path that today carries the research teams to Chauvet Cave.

Once the location, size and shape of the Pleistocene cave entrance was worked out, the key question became when and how it had closed, losing its distant visibility. This was determined principally through cosmogenic ^{36}Cl dating (see Link 7, available as supplementary material at www.cambridge.org/mobilelands-capes) of the current cliff-face immediately above the cave, along with boulders from the massive rockfall that now seals the entrance. The results showed that the Pleistocene entrance had closed through a sequence of three major collapses of the limestone escarpment. The first took place 29,400 ± 1,800 years ago, the second 23,500 ± 1,200 years ago and the third 21,500 ± 1,000 years ago (Sadier et al. 2012:8004–5). These cosmogenic ages directly on the rock of the collapsed escarpment are consistent with the ages of archaeological materials inside the cave, such as piles of stocked charcoal, charcoal torch marks on the walls and charcoal paintings in the cave, all of which pre-date the last rockfall event that finally sealed the cave. All of the bones of large fauna in the cave are also older than the final rock collapse of 21,500 ± 1,000 years ago, indicating that by then the cave had finally ceased to be accessible by both people and large animals (Quiles et al. 2016:4674; Sadier et al. 2012:8005). It had also disappeared from view (Figure 10). How, then, can we imagine its place in a landscape traversed and occupied by people throughout the Upper Palaeolithic?

To answer that question, we need to understand the broader landscape, and to do so we need to consider its various landforms across the region. Of course, there are potentially infinite numbers of things to consider: the trees and other elements of the vegetation, their types, densities, seasonal variability, community structure, potential resources and the like; and geological landforms, their shapes, sizes, proximity to archaeological sites and degrees of inter-visibility across the land-scape. To disentangle key factors to focus on among this complex network of potentially relevant environmental details, we ask 'what makes this place differ-ent to other areas nearby?', and 'does anything stand out that would draw a person's attention?'. Is there anything in those differences, in both questions, that would act like beacons by which to draw attention to the cave, or that would position the cave favourably in relation to the broader environment?

Chauvet Cave has an unusual richness of unique and regionally defining features. Prominent among these is the Pont d'Arc archway above the Ardèche River, looking out onto the cave and vice versa. But did it exist at the time of the

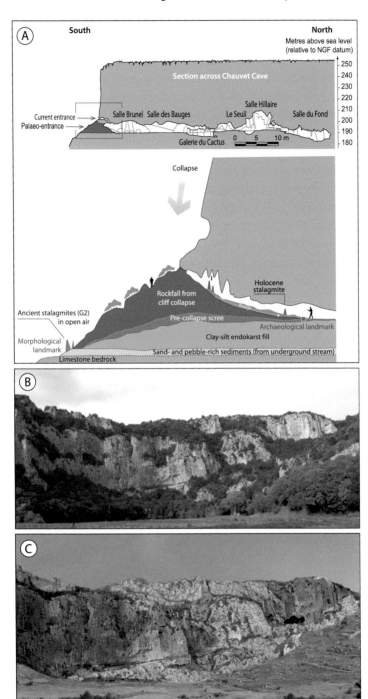

Figure 10 The sealing of the Upper Palaeolithic entrance of Chauvet Cave.
(A) Collapse of the limestone escarpment left a massive rockfall talus that

cave's occupation, or has it formed since? This question has frequently been raised by researchers, with some even seeing a similarity, and with this a symbolic connection, between the shape of the archway and the ventral arch of woolly mammoths as drawn on the walls of the cave (Clottes 2018:399–400). This potential similarity aside, the presence of the distinctive, visually prominent archway across the relic Combe d'Arc meander adds to the location's ability to draw attention, interconnect with an unusual and prominent landform and render a sense of place.

To address these questions, the antiquity of the Pont d'Arc archway was investigated by studying its geomorphology along with that of the abandoned meander and various other alluvial terraces nearby. A fine-grained three-dimensional geophysical survey of each of these landscape features was undertaken to determine how their formation histories articulated through time. It revealed that prior to c. 124,000 years ago, the Ardèche River flowed alongside the now-relic meander, bypassing the archway. The river then left the meander of the Cirque d'Estre to flow through the arch of Pont d'Arc, whose morphology was then somewhat shallower than it is today, as the river had previously largely bypassed it (Genuite et al. 2021). The significant conclusion here is that the river had already long flowed through the archway by the time people began to occupy Chauvet Cave, and the Combe d'Arc meander was already dry land, having long been abandoned by the river by the time the cave was first used. By then, the landforms outside the cave were much as they are today, although exactly what they meant to people then is anybody's guess. The layout of the gorge, with its river flowing through a giant archway framed by a towering amphitheatre-shaped limestone cliff-line, enabled the cave's wide-open entrance to be easily seen from either side of the archway (Figure 11).

It is no coincidence that the Ardèche River's network of colossal gorges houses the largest complex of Upper Palaeolithic cave art sites in southeastern France, with Chauvet Cave being the richest of them all in terms of the number of individual works of art and complexity of their panels (Delannoy et al. 2013). This is also a region whose limestone cliff-lines guided and facilitated travel

---

Caption for Figure 10 (cont.)

sealed the cave entrance. (B) The Chauvet Cave cliff-line as seen from the Comb d'Arc meander today. (C) Reconstruction of the Chauvet Cave cliff-line at the time of its occupation c. 34,500–37,500 cal BP. The vegetation reconstruction is based on a combination of pollen analyses and the identification of wood charcoal found in the cave (figure by Jean-Jacques Delannoy and Stephane Jaillet).

Figure 11 Evolution of the meander of the Ardèche River and opening of the Pont d'Arc archway c. 124,000 years ago. The physical landscape depicted here is visually much like it would have been known by the people of Chauvet Cave during the two main phases of occupation. Some 158,000 years ago, the Ardèche River flowed around the Pont d'Arc landform, signalling that the archway did not yet exist. Around 124,000 years ago, the river began to change direction, flowing through the newly formed archway. When the river level was high, water spilled into the thalweg (the lowest-lying course) of the older river channel (after Genuite et al. 2021).

across the landscape by physically constraining the flat, open spaces along the river's banks. In doing so, cliff-base travel along the river banks connected numerous cave entrances across the landscape.

The intervisibility of dominant features, such as the archway at Pont d'Arc, the prominent Chauvet Cave entrance and individual features of the high cliffs, facilitated navigation, drawing the onlooker along a well-marked landscape that would have acted as anticipated landscape-scale beacons along well-defined travel routes. But it is only by understanding which of these features of the landscape existed at the time of interest that their relevance to the archaeological landscape can emerge.

3.1.3 The Physical Accessibility of Archaeological Sites

Caves often have unusually rich pre- and post-occupational deposits underground: rock collapses and anthropic modifications and installations on their floors; evidence of taphonomic reworkings; and, on their walls, formations such as mineral skins that may reveal environmental details of interest for the period(s) of human occupation or for the dating of underlying or overlying rock art (e.g. David et al. 2017; Delannoy 2018; see also e.g. Green et al. 2021).

Cave spaces are thus ripe for study. By examining how a site was materially configured and provisioned through time, archaeology and geomorphology can together reveal its *spatial history*.

Sealed sites such as Cosquer Cave and Chauvet Cave often preserve exceptional remnants of the past. This is because exogenous taphonomic disturbances such as rainfall, wind, animals and people are more limited or entirely eliminated once entryways are blocked. Sometimes, such as at Chauvet Cave, the footprints and handprints of people and pawprints of animals going back tens of thousands of years are preserved, impressed into the floors' soft sediments. And if we can see such traces of the past today, so too will they have been visible to people in the past. The cultural story of a cave concerns not just when its various features were made but also all later engagements, for once something exists, it has the potential to influence subsequent perceptions and interpretations, and with this, what people did there. The careful mapping and documentation of a site enables the researcher to establish what was there when, as a precondition to understanding what and sometimes why various activities took place. These, too, are elements of enduring places, and inform the experiences of human mobility between, and their return to, places.

For example, at Chauvet Cave the presence of well-preserved human and animal footprints is now well known. What is less well recognised is that they are only found in particular sectors of the cave, not in others. Their absence from most of the cave can be used to frame key questions. The superb preservation of certain types of archaeological materials and marks in some parts of the cave can create a false perception that everything has remained intact, as in the 'Pompeii premise' discussed in Section 2 (cf. Binford 1981; Schiffer 1985). Yet careful on-site observation and the transdisciplinary mapping of the cave's floor, in this case undertaken at a 1:50 scale, has made it possible to identify a whole raft of modifications. Some were caused by human actions, others were not; some are subtle and probably insignificant, others are more obvious. Material remains and traces on the ground, walls or ceiling can help position past activities in relative chronological sequence, depending on which lies over or under the other. Similarly, evidence for the repeated use of specific areas, such as pathways used many times, can shed light on normative or planned activities (see Section 4). Here we give two examples of how understanding changes in the physical configuration of the cave has helped better understand why archaeological materials are spatially structured as they are: (1) the closure of the cave mouth; and (2) the growth of extensive speleothem formations in some chambers and passageways.

We have already noted how the cave's wide and high, domed entrance completely closed c. 21,500 years ago as a result of multiple escarpment collapses. By constructing a three-dimensional model of the cave and its external environment, including the precise size and shape of its entrance, it became possible to work out how far into the cave daylight penetrated when the palaeo-entrance was open (Figure 12). The presence and intensity of penetrating light had often been raised by researchers, for such knowledge appeared to be necessary to better understand the differential distribution of paintings on the walls and ceiling, and of the installations on the floors of the many chambers in this massive network of narrow corridors and open chambers.

The three-dimensional model enabled the penetration of subdued sunlight, and areas of shadow and darkness, to be mapped and envisioned in relation to the cave's archaeological features (Figure 12). Inside the cave, people had stuck Cave Bear femur bones at intervals into the floor of what is now the Great Hall of Les Bauges (Figure 13) (Debard et al. 2020:210–1). The alignment of the vertically planted bones marked the transition zone between what were then areas of semi-darkness and full darkness. Such information is not just peripheral for our current understanding of what happened in the past. Rather, it also helps understand why some parts of the cave have few or no signs of people, despite their clayey-loamy floors being conducive to good preservation. Hence, in proximal parts of the cave where sunlight once reached, the rockfall that saw the closure of the cave functioned, and continues to function, as a conduit for rainwater to flow across the cave floor. The percolating water infiltrates the mass of blocks onto the now-sealed entrance chamber, erasing the signs of human and animal movements and activities from the floor. But further away, in more protected areas, the rich traces of human and animal activities on the floors of other chambers and passageways remain. They are thus given a new context by which to better interpret what can still be seen in the cave today. These details enable researchers to better pinpoint those sectors where the 'original' surfaces remain more or less intact (Figure 14).

The question of what Chauvet Cave was like in the deep past also arises with regard to its abundant speleothems. Visually, many white and sparkly stalagmites, columns, flowstones, rim-pools and shawls contrast with the dull brown of the clayey floors. They date to different times, with the most recent generations of concretions dating to long after the closure of the cave. Post-dating the period of human occupation by thousands of years, they are, therefore, irrelevant to its occupational history (Genty et al. 2020; Quiles et al. 2016; Sadier et al. 2020; Valladas et al. 2020a, 2020b, 2020c, 2020d). Those speleothems should thus not feature in reconstructions of the Upper Palaeolithic cave landscape, but this would not be known had the more recent

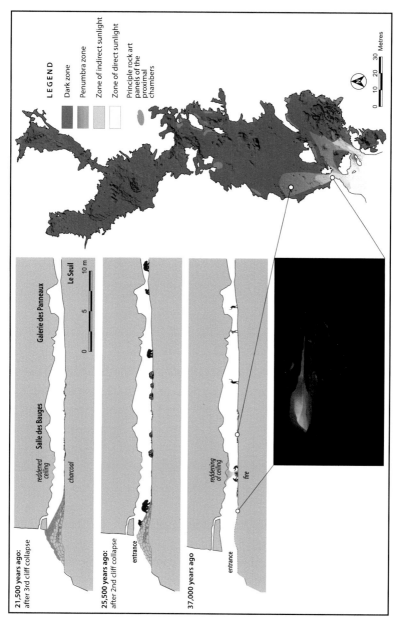

Figure 12 Modelling the penetration of sunlight from the Upper Palaeolithic entrance of Chauvet Cave. The model was produced using terrestrial LiDAR (figure by Jean-Jacques Delannoy; 3D model Kim Genuite).

Figure 13 Examples of two Cave Bear femurs planted in the ground of the Great Hall of Les Bauges. A series of such Cave Bear femurs were planted vertically along the edge of the liminal zone beyond which indirect sunlight does not reach. They are thought to demarcate the edge of the visible passageway from the entrance chamber as it gives way to the Great Hall of Les Bauges deeper inside the cave, the first large but pitch-black chamber of Chauvet Cave (photos by Julien Monney).

speleothems not been dated and their chronologies worked out. Combining the archaeology with the geomorphology, together aided by the construction of 3D models and detailed maps, now enables us to imagine what the cave looked like some 34,500–37,500 cal BP, at the time when its first paintings were made (Figures 12 and 14). The cave did not have its present lustrous surfaces, but rather a more sombre tint dominated by clayey-loamy floors. The digital removal of the Holocene concretions from the cave's current internal landscape highlights how some of its chambers had different configurations, opening up new directions of research (Figure 15).

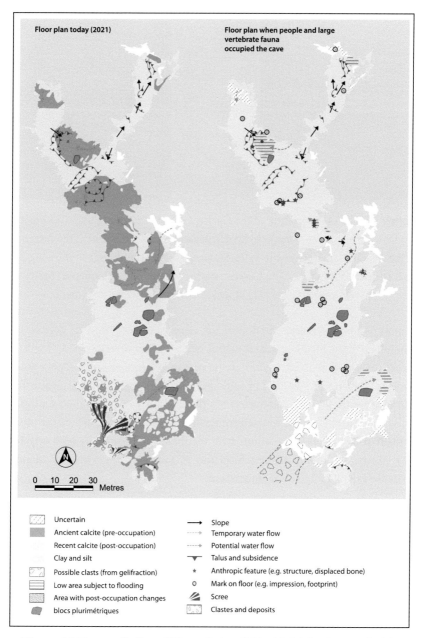

Figure 14 Current (left) and Upper Palaeolithic (right) landscapes inside Chauvet Cave.

As a last example of how understanding the palaeo-landscape inside the cave enables better understanding of its archaeology is the absence of paintings in the entrance zone once reached by indirect sunlight. The detailed

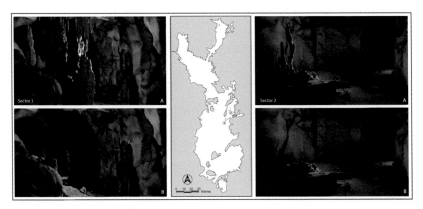

Figure 15 The configuration of the Cactus Gallery, Chauvet Cave. (A) Today.
(B) During the time of both periods of occupation. Left: In Sector 1, the entrance
of the Cactus Gallery from the Salle des Bauges. Right: In Sector 2, showing the
rock structure known as 'The Cactus', partly a result of roof collapse, partly of
human construction (3D model courtesy of Benjamin Sadier).

geomorphological reconstruction of the cave's entrance, and its digital 3D
modelling, show that the rock art begins where the sunlight stopped. Opening
up the cave entrance and digitally removing the Holocene speleothems gives
a much better understanding of why there is an absence of paintings in the
entrance zones, precisely to the extremities of the reach of subdued sunlight.
This is of particular value to archaeologists, for we now know where the more
hidden art is, and its associations with the more liminal spaces both physically and experientially distant from the everyday, sunlit world of human
settlements and daily social interaction.

3.2 Conclusion

A site may well be what holds the artefacts, paintings or bone and pollen
sequences, for example, but it is its broader landscape setting that enables it to
be understood as part of the larger world in which people structured their lives.
Archaeologists and their associated Quaternary science research teams are well
used to studying past vegetation communities through pollen cores, faunal assemblages and sediment sequences for what they can tell about the environments of the
past. They also frequently involve geomorphological investigations to interpret
rockfalls and other kinds of sediment build-up and taphonomic processes. Less
common are fine-grained studies aimed at determining precisely what a site and its
surrounding landscape was like at the time of its occupation. The two examples of
Cosquer Cave and Chauvet Cave are interesting because they temper an impression of stability implied by their superb states of preservation with evidence of

significant change. The attention to detail is key: only detailed morphogenic reconstructions encompassing multiple, and often fine-grained, characteristics of the site and its surrounds can provide a precise image of the state of the lived environment at the time the caves were occupied.

3.3 Further Readings

Clottes, J., Courtin, J. & Vanrell, L. (2005). *Cosquer Redécouvert*. Paris: Seuil.

Delannoy, J.-J. & Geneste, J.-M. (Eds.) (2020). *Monographie de la Grotte Chauvet-Pont d'Arc: Volume 1 – Atlas de la Grotte Chauvet-Pont d'Arc*. Paris: Documents de l'Archéologie Française, Éditions de la Maison des Sciences de l'Homme.

Lacroix, D., Bell, T., Shaw, J. & Westley, K. (2014). Submerged archaeological landscapes and the recording of precontact history: Examples from Atlantic Canada. In Evans, A. M., Flatman, J. C. & Flemming, N. C. (Eds.), *Prehistoric Archaeology on the Continental Shelf*, pp. 13–35. New York: Springer.

Lichter, M., Zviely, D., Klein, M. & Sivan, D. (2010). Sea-level changes in the Mediterranean: Past, present, and future – A review. In Israel, A., Einav, R. & Seckbach, J. (Eds.), *Seaweeds and Their Role in Globally Changing Environments*, pp. 3–17. Dordrecht: Springer.

Olive, M. & Vanrell, L. (2021). La caverne et ses différents espaces. In Vanrell, L. & Olive, M. (Eds.), *La Grotte Cosquer: Trente Ans de Recherches*. Dossiers d'Archéologie 408:26–9.

Quiles, A., Valladas, H., Bocherens, H., et al. (2016). A high-precision chronological model for the decorated Upper Paleolithic cave of Chauvet-Pont d'Arc, Ardèche, France. *Proceedings of the National Academy of Sciences of the United States of America* 113(17):4670–5. https://doi.org/10.1073/pnas.1523158113.

4 Mappings: Archaeomorphology and the Created Environment

In Section 3, we discussed the importance of reconstructing a site's environmental setting in as much detail as possible, so that the contexts of the choices people made can be better understood. Such palaeoenvironmental reconstructions are typically based on a combination of geomorphological (e.g. sediment formation) and palaeo-biogeographic (e.g. pollen, animal bone, aDNA) archives from archaeological sites and their surroundings. This information is sometimes integrated into 3D models to reconstruct, visualise and study the palaeo-landscapes. However, these same archives can also be interrogated in another way: for how people in the past actively constructed, used and managed their environments. Here the notion of *engagement* is useful: how did people materially interact with each other and with everything else around them, *actively creating* their landscapes in the process? In this section we explore how to examine anthropic signs of created landscapes from the material world, for it is this that enables us to approach a site and its landscape through such a 'building perspective'. The particularities of human engagements with things result in very particular archaeological and geomorphological signatures. In other words, palaeoenvironments, and the archaeological record, are not just products of responses to climate change or to the geomorphological and biogeographic conditions of the day. Rather, they are actively constructed in relationships between people and with the things they interact with (Lock 2000).

Precisely how people engaged with the things around them, constructing their environments in the process, can be worked out by analysing the physical traces of human actions at sites and in the broader landscape. Here we outline a method for studying how people 'made' the caves and rockshelters they inhabited – not just how they used them but also more critically how they shaped them as structured, meaningful places suited to their needs and cultural mores. At some sites, people will have left few traces, and the evidence of past engagements will therefore be sparse. An example is where a single block of rock has been moved a few metres. But at other sites the evidence will be overwhelming. Once that evidence comes to light, we may as well speak of their *architectural* design, refurbishment and of created environments, because of the visibility of the human hand in their formation and planning (e.g. David et al. 2018; Delannoy et al. 2017; Jaubert et al. 2016; Ontañon 2003; see also Theunissen et al. 1998). In each case, what are implicated are the thoughts and social gestures of people acted out in their place-worlds (for the notion of the 'place-world', see Casey 1993, 1996).

Working out precisely what these gestures were, and when they took place at a site, requires being able to identify the material traces of human actions. To do so requires examining the morphologies of sites and distinguishing how they changed over time as a result of both human (anthropogenic) actions and non-anthropogenic site formation processes.[2] For the latter, it is essential to determine

---

[2] We distinguish between 'anthropogenic' and 'anthropic' throughout this Element. 'Anthropogenic' refers to the direct outcomes of human actions; 'anthropic' to any kind of human-induced outcome, direct or indirect. An example of an anthropogenic outcome is when a person intentionally or accidently moves a rock in a cave (e.g. by picking it up or kicking it as they walk). An example of an indirect, anthropic outcome is when a low rock overhang collapses years after campfires were lit underneath it, as a result of its repeated drying, contraction and expansion as people came and went, developing stress fractures and becoming weakened by the heat of the fires over time (the concepts of 'natural' versus 'cultural' site formation processes can

whether changes to the contents and shape of a site are contemporaneous or subsequent to its human occupation, as determined by the archaeology, oral traditions, historical archives and so on (see Section 3). Distinguishing between anthropogenic and non-anthropogenic modifications of the physical matrix of a site is a major aim of *archaeomorphology* (a conjuction of 'archaeology' and 'geomorphology'), as described next.

Archaeomorphology as a way of studying places simultaneously works in two ways: conceptual and methodological. Conceptually, a site is approached by thinking of it as part of the place-world of human lives. By approaching a site as a place invested with life through how it is culturally conceived and socially engaged – by how it is used, shaped and reshaped by human actions – it becomes amenable to archaeological enquiry for what it can reveal about those actions and, with this, about the cultural past. That 'archaeological' enquiry in reality makes use of all the other disciplinary techniques better known to geomorphology, pollen analysis, palaeontology, palaeoecology and so on, and that together make for transdisciplinary research (see Section 1). 'Archaeomorphology' is the term we use when archaeology and geomorphology come together in this way.

Currently most research on site formation processes tends to focus on so-called natural processes (e.g. for caves and rockshelters, rockfall, exfoliation of rock surfaces, formation of speleothems etc.; for soft floor sediments at all kinds of sites, erosion, deposition and the reworking of sediments by the elements, plants and animals; and transport by wind, water and gravity). Yet over what have now been many decades, researchers have also repeatedly pointed out that in many instances human actions have caused sites to cumulatively grow as they were progressively engaged. This latter concern has been coined a 'building perspective' (McFadyen 2008). Despite this awareness, too rarely is the role of people in site formation systematically pursued, unless the site itself was obviously assembled by people, such as in wooden, shaped stone or mudbrick structures. Nevertheless, in recent years caves and rockshelters, traditionally seen as the epitomy of 'natural' formations that conveniently offered shelter to people and animals, have also started to be viewed from a building perspective. Examples are Chauvet Cave (Delannoy et al. 2013) and Bruniquel (Jaubert et al. 2016) in France, La Garma in Spain (Ontañon 2003) and Nawarla Gabarnmang (David et al. 2018; Delannoy et al. 2017) and Borologa 1 (Delannoy et al. 2020b; Genuite et al. 2021) in Australia. Thinking from the outset about these sites as places built, occupied and modified by their occupants makes for a more

---

become blurred when dealing with notions of dwelling and inhabitation; see Ingold (2000) and Thomas (2008)).

nuanced way of conceiving of, studying and visualising the cultural dimensions of place. It is their stories we explore next.

How, then, can the 'building' dimension of a 'building perspective' be systematically investigated for enduring places that began prior to their first human occupations, and among caves and rockshelters in particular? This is the task of archaeomorphology, which aims to work out who and what caused all aspects of a site's materiality to have become what it is through time. Such a research agenda requires analysis of a site's individual features at high spatial resolution. The position and antiquity of each object, each surface and each 'empty space' is interrogated. Each item at a site – such as a cupule on a wall, broken stalactite on a ceiling, broken speleothem or isolated rock on the ground or depression in the floor – is investigated for how it came to be there and how it attained its features in that site as an active, continually transforming three-dimensional space. During the course of such investigations, some things come to be seen as 'out of place': a broken stalactite some distance from where it would have fallen (*if* it had fallen); an isolated rectangular-shaped rock slab whose edges all run across rather than follow fracture planes or lines of weakness and so on. The recognition of such objects of interest for a building perspective is based on the detailed study of all that is present and visible in the studied site. Each object has significance in the site's formation history, produc-ing the landscape within the site, and therefore requires inspection for how it came to be where it is today. Nothing is the result of chance. Every object, however small, can carry information on the processes that caused it to be how and where it is within (or out of) a site. The detailed examination of different kinds of physical objects and spaces ('empty' spaces also require explanation) makes it possible to apprehend or mentally capture not only the mark of human hands but also what could not have gotten there without people. The question then becomes how, and when, were people involved, and how does this relate to other contemporary traces of human activity nearby.

To shed further light on this approach, we begin with some key concepts behind the major tool of archaeomorphological analysis: mapping.

4.1 Approaching the Archaeology of Place Through Cartography

Archaeomorphology engages as many different disciplines and methods as war-ranted, as checks and cross-checks on ideas and results, and to 'cable' the evidence for a stronger outcome (on 'cabling', see Bernstein 1983:69; Wylie 1989).

Archaeomorphology is fundamentally an integrative, transdisciplinary approach that explores archaeological sites regardless of their dimensions, specificities or uses. Its underlying principle is that each discipline brings to the table specialised knowledge that feeds back onto the others, extending each other's realm of enquiry in the process. It is not so much the contribution of one discipline or another that is important, but their integration in a unified approach that together goes beyond the limitations of each, and that thus results in more than the sum of the parts.

Archaeomorphological mapping was first attempted at Chauvet Cave in the Ardèche region of France. The cave's discovery in 1994 quickly alerted archaeologists and, soon after, the general public of its great significance, both because of its rich and often complex rock art, and its great age (see Section 3). A transdisciplinary team was soon after brought together to investigate the cave's deep-time history. The research focus were the traces of the past left on its floors and on its walls, more so than what was buried underground. Some thirty years later, what we now know about the cave is largely based on the careful mapping of all the objects and marks that lie on the ground and on the walls. Each item and surface was carefully examined for what it can tell us about how the cave was engaged.

As already noted, a key tool of archaeomorphology is cartography (Delannoy & Geneste 2020; Delannoy et al. 2001, 2017). Through careful observation, archaeomorphology brings together the details of a site's morphology, its marks and individual objects and their causes of transport onto a single, integrated map. Given the many kinds of details evident at a site, and at rich sites such as Chauvet Cave in particular, and the need to not disturb or dissociate the various traces of people's actions from other site contexts, the cartographic work first needed to establish a series of protocols systematically defining and visually differentiating between the different kinds of information it could amass. To make this possible, three parameters were required: (1) the space to be mapped needed to be defined (floors, walls, etc.); (2) a high-resolution topographic base map that would enable individual objects and features of the cave's three-dimensional surfaces to be differentiated had to be drawn; and (3) The logic of a legend systematically capturing the full range of spatial details about the site's archaeology and geomorphology had to be defined (see Link 8, available as supplementary material at www.cambridge .org/mobilelandscapes).

For Chauvet Cave, the most important space to be mapped was the floor. This may at first seem paradoxical given that the cave is best known for the art on its walls. Yet the archaeomorphological map needs to integrate complex details of the cave's three-dimensional space. The sediments on the floor constitute a rich common denominator for the research fields involved in the study of the site, one where different kinds of information could merge. They contain evidence of the presence and movements of both animals and people, in the form of animal tracks and human footprints, for example. Bioturbation, caused by the animals who trampled the mud and shifted objects as they moved through the cave, was most evident on the ground. Human structures and modifications, such as hearths, clay extraction pits and installations made of rocks and broken speleothems, were also most evident on the floors. And here, too, were signs of the hydrological and other environmental processes that had affected the distribution and preservation of archaeological remains across the cave. The floor sediments also retained details of transformations that had taken place after the period of human occupation, such as the development of speleothems, run-off and displacement and fossilisation of archaeological and palaeontological remains. As with more standard archaeological site maps, the floors were therefore of fundamental importance when recording the details of what had happened in the cave when people were there, including the taphonomic evidence that enables its palaeo-condition to be better understood. To account for all these aspects, a systematic code needed to be developed for the cartographic work, as represented in the map's legend. Given the complexity of the recorded details, which includes both spatial and temporal dimensions, each set of morphogenic process represented on the map was given its own colour code (Figures 16 and 17; see Link 8, available as supplementary material at www.cambridge.org/mobilelandscapes for further details). To account for the element of time, the darker the shading on the map, the more recent the mapped feature or process was, so that the passage of time could itself be represented.

Seven main processes are captured on the floor map, and eighty-two types of objects are distinguished. They are all systematically differentiated in the legend (see Link 8, available as supplementary material at www.cambridge .org/mobilelandscapes). It was also essential to link the objects visible on the floor with the anthropic marks on the walls and ceilings (rock art, torch marks, scrapings of clay, extracted rocks, broken stalactites etc.). Details of where parts of the wall had fallen or been artificially removed onto the ground were shown on the map through vertical projections visually represented by square symbols (Figure 16). Through such cartographic codes, three-dimensional details incorporating multiple kinds of information (e.g. geomorphic, archaeological) and the movement of objects through time, with their causes identified, could be shown on a single map (Figure 17). If reading such a complex map seems difficult, it is due to the richness and complexity of the site – the map is at once an abstraction and simplification that isolates and highlights what is relevant to the question at hand, and the bringing together and cross-correlation of multiple lines of evidence. Like all maps, the Chauvet Cave archaeomorphological map is an abstraction that redacts while integrating a large amount of connected

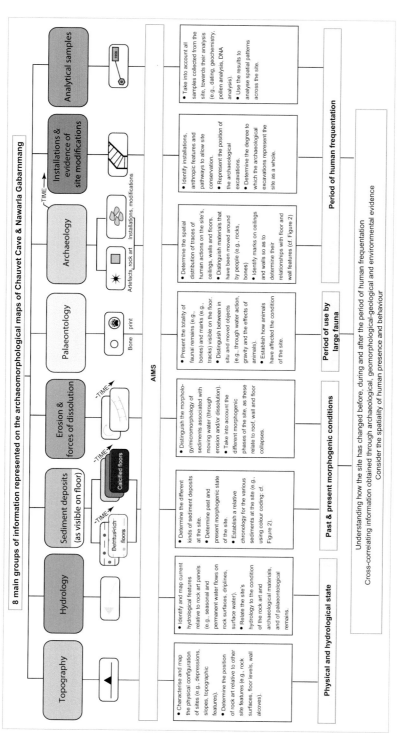

Figure 16 The main groups of information recorded on the Chauvet Cave maps (figure by Jean-Jacques Delannoy).

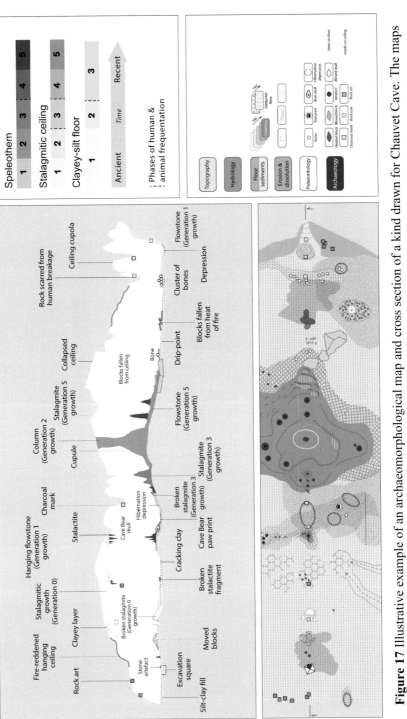

Figure 17 Illustrative example of an archaeomorphological map and cross section of a kind drawn for Chauvet Cave. The maps integrate multiple lines of evidence on the site's geomorphic and anthropic site formation processes through time (figure by Jean-Jacques Delannoy).

information into a single graphic. This is precisely the aim of the map: to report on 'everything' at the site so that the multi-disciplinary evidence of its three-dimensional space – incorporating objects, surfaces, processes and time – can all be connected. It aims to give a more dynamic rendition of the past than the more conventional two-dimensional maps currently do. Its aim is to not over-simplify what is being represented by erasing critical contextual information, so that the complexity and dynamism of the site's formation can be read. Again, it is important to remember that in mapping generally, each abstraction is a simplification that filters out what is there but not shown. It is an erasure of what is deemed not important for the task at hand, but in doing so can easily fall into the trap of silencing essential information on the mapped site's formation history, its movements, its contemporaneous and non-contemporaneous presences and transformations. With this in mind, incorporating into the Chauvet Cave map as many details and dimensions of its three-dimensional space and formation processes as possible both resulted from and recursively further enabled the various disciplinary lines of evidence to be cross-correlated. Such a process of investigation is much more difficult and less capable of reaching cross-disciplinary results when limited to simplified maps that separately cover individual themes and disciplines as more or less isolated phenomena.

Finally, archaeomorphological mapping is also a most effective way of acquiring information from a site: as each object is observed in the making of the map, and irrespective of its size, it can be associated with the process(es) that caused it to be where it is, making it possible to explain its position, arrangement, present state and temporality, both in terms of when it came to be formed and the transformations that took place since. By integrating these multiple dimensions, mapping itself becomes an act of knowledge creation.

This same cartographic approach has now been applied to other archaeological sites around the world, both in the open air (e.g. Delannoy et al. 2022) and underground (e.g. Jaillet & Monney 2018). Depending on the site and research questions asked, the map and its legend can be adapted and enriched with additional cartographic symbols that befit the situation at hand, all the while retaining its logic of integration of multiple lines of information towards transdisciplinary research (see Link 9, available as supplementary material at www.cambridge.org/mobilelandscapes).

4.2 Archaeological Sites as Architectural Spaces

There are many ways in which people in the past inscribed their presence and activities in the landscape, notably by building and modifying things. At some sites, individual blocks of rock were displaced, such as to form steps along passageways. At others, activity areas were demarcated by removing rocks to create clear spaces, or by adding rock alignments, for example. Objects that were accidently displaced by people or animals while moving across a site are themselves evidence of frequentation, even in the case of fleeting events. In the following examples, only voluntary anthropogenic acts of modification are addressed, keeping in mind that accidental traces can also be present, mapped and investigated. The recognition, reading and understanding of both kinds of evidence are in each case facilitated by archaeomorphological mapping.

4.2.1 The Movement and Arrangement of Blocks on the Floor

Stone arrangements in open sites have long been recorded by archaeologists around the world, such as 'megaliths' and rock cairns in Europe (e.g. Laporte et al. 2022), or standing stones and rock alignments in Australia (e.g. Delannoy et al. 2020a). In contrast, it is only recently that archaeologists have paid much attention to unobtrusive rock structures in caves and rockshelters. This is largely because rockfall and outcropping bedrock can easily mask moved rocks, especially when the stone arrangements consist of single rocks or small and unremarkable piles made of unmodified blocks (Figure 18). Identifying such anthropogenic structures – that is, distinguishing them from rockfall and the like – often comes not from a targetting of the constructions themselves, but from the high-resolution mapping of all features in a site. When mapping is undertaken, objects are carefully observed in the field, so that sets of rocks which at first appear part of the natural landscape become differentiated as their finer details and spatial contexts become apparent: a particular rock may be isolated on the ground, without traces of rock collapse overhead or on the ground, and without any other obvious way of having reached its current position other than by having been carried there by people. Or an isolated rock may have come from a particular stratum of a rockshelter's outcrop, but without any part of that rock layer being exposed in the bedrock nearby; how, then, did it get there? Flaking scars may indicate that some rocks were removed from larger blocks or from the outcropping bedrock. By identifying how each rock attained its current shape, or where its geological source (the outcropping rock layer) relative to the rock in question is, the cause of creation and positioning of each object can be worked out (Figure 19). A search for the exact source of a rock can then be undertaken. This is done by recording its particular characteristics such as dimensions, lithology, flaking scars and other surface characteristics that can then be matched to its originating source, including through conjoining (by manually moving the rock if deemed appropriate, or digitally following three-dimensional scanning of movable objects

Figure 18 Examples of manually constructed installations in French, Australian and Canadian caves and rockshelters. (A) A large limestone block placed at the bottom of a jump-down makes a step for the descent from the entrance tunnel into Cloggs Cave's main chamber (Australia). (B) Isolated block positioned in a hollow along a slippery section of a passage at Chauvet Cave (France). We know that this section of the passageway was particularly slippery because Cave Bear slippage marks can be seen on the floor. The step implies planned, repeated travel along the passageway. (C) Semi-infilled activity area delimited by imported rocks. The encircling rocks came from the outer edges of the Chuchuwayha rockshelter (British Columbia, Canada). (D) Collapsed stool. The five blocks were stacked to enable its user to flake and/or paint the ceiling along the outer edge of Nawarla Gabarnmang (Arnhem Land, Australia). (E) Set of twelve standing stones positioned at the intersection of two chambers at Chauvet Cave. (F) Three longitudinally aligned flowstone blocks extracted from another part of Chauvet Cave. Clay was caked as a filler to seal the gaps between the joints, signalling its probable use as an artificial basin (photos A, C and D by Jean-Jacques Delannoy; photos B, E and F by Stéphane Jaillet).

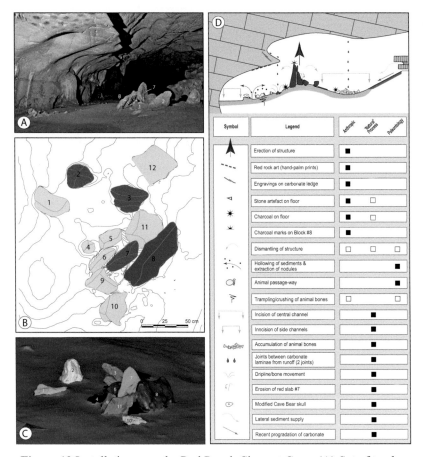

Figure 19 Installation near the Red Panel, Chauvet Cave. (A) Set of twelve standing stones arranged at the intersection of two chambers. (B) Bird's-eye view of the installation showing the layout of the now-partially collapsed standing stones. (C) 3D model of the stone arrangement. (D) Legend that includes information on both the materials and processes of formation and dismantlement by people and animals (photo, cartography and 3D model by Stéphane Jaillet, compilation by Jean-Jacques Delannoy).

and bedrock surfaces). Such a matching of a moved rock to its parent surface is facilitated by detailed knowledge of all the rock formations within and near the site; here, too, the detailed mapping of an entire landscape, of a site and its surroundings, helps. This is precisely how the origin of displaced blocks was worked out at Chauvet Cave, and at Cloggs Cave (Delannoy et al. 2020a) and Borologa (Delannoy et al. 2020b) in Australia (Figure 18A).

At Chauvet Cave and Borologa, some of the rocks had been moved up to about 10 m across the landscape (Figure 20). Their purposes are not always known, but

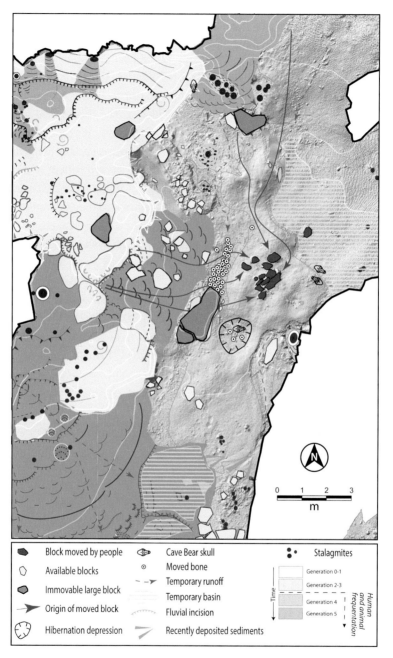

Figure 20 Provenance of the blocks that make up the installation near the Red Panel, Chauvet Cave (figure by Jean-Jacques Delannoy and Stéphane Jaillet).

some signal pathways (the rocks having been used to form steps across impediments), water-retention devices (enclosures for basins), stools by which to reach high areas (piled slabs) or spatial markers and reference points (cairns). At Chuchuwayha, a granite rockshelter in British Columbia (Canada), archaeomorphological mapping made it possible to distinguish disparate anthropogenic rock configurations amongst an immense chaos of blocks. The totality had largely resulted from successive wall and ceiling collapses, but from the rockfall people had removed some blocks to create distinctive social spaces such as living areas and burial locations, each activity area demarcated by its own pattern of moved blocks creating a distinctive open space (Figure 18C). Without the archaeomorphological mapping, some of those spaces, and their moved blocks, would have gone unnoticed. At other sites, stone arrangements marked important places, such as a set of subtly erected rocks wedged together in an alcove at Cloggs Cave in GunaiKurnai Aboriginal Country, Australia. A few metres away, a now-buried slab naturally shaped like the profile of a bird was erected on the palaeo-floor c. 2,000 cal BP. We only know of it today because it was revealed when this part of the site was archaeologically excavated (David et al. 2021a, 2021b) (Figure 21).

However, archaeomorphological mapping does more than enable activity areas and anthropogenic installations to be identified. Perhaps more importantly, it enables sites to be analysed through a 'building perspective', by reverse

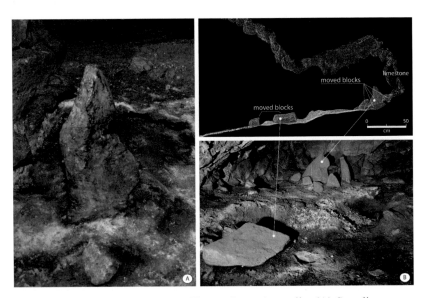

Figure 21 Stone arrangements at Cloggs Cave, Australia. (A) Standing stone erected c. 2,000 cal BP and subsequently buried by accumulating soft sediments. (B) Undated stone arrangement in 'the Alcove' inside the cave.

engineering the *chaîne opératoire* or sequence of steps taken to construct its installations or cavities, for example. At Chauvet Cave, the blocks making up two stone installations – one a step, the other demarcating the edge of a basin – came not from the local bedrock, which is difficult to extract without modern metal tools given its hardness and lack of cracks and fissures. Rather, the step and materials forming the edge of the basin were made of more easily breakable, thick stalagmitic floors perched c. 1 m above ground level, c. 20 m from the most distant of the two installations (Delannoy & Geneste 2020) (Figures 18B and 18F).

While our research has focused on the rocks, the same reasoning can also be applied to the animal bones found on the floor of Chauvet Cave. In many cases their position on the ground does not correspond with where the animals died. In some places, skeletal parts had been moved away from the rest of the skeleton. Sometimes this was due to taphonomic factors such as the action of flowing water, but at other times people are clearly implicated. Thus, inside the cave, Cave Bear femurs were planted in the ground, apparently to trace a passage deeper into the cave where much rock art is found on its walls (see Section 3). Elsewhere in the cave, a Cave Bear skull was placed on a flat-topped block that had collapsed from the roof. The block-with-skull was itself surrounded by some fifty other Cave Bear skulls (Monney et al. 2020) (Figure 22). Clearly, the block with the skull, and the large open chamber that houses it was once a focus of human activity (Montelle 2022).

4.2.2 Speleothems: The Meaningfulness of Raw Materials

In limestone caves, speleothems such as stalactites, stalagmites and columns are often important features of the subterranean landscape. Today they are the things that usually feature in tourist caves and photographs. This fascination with speleothems is not new: in Europe, during the eighteenth and nineteenth centuries, when cave tourism became popular, it was common for visitors to break and take calcite concretions home as trophies of their visits to remarkable places (Issartel 2008).

But the breaking of stalagmites and stalactites by people also has a much longer history. At Bruniquel in France, 336 m deep into the limestone cave and in pitch-black conditions requiring artificial fires for lighting, as far back as c. 176,500 ± 2,100 years ago Neanderthals had broken stalagmites and repositioned them into circular arrangements (Jaubert et al. 2016; Leveque & Mora 2021; Verheyden et al. 2016) (Figures 23A and 23B). At La Garma in Spain and at the Cave of Saint Marcel d'Ardèche in France, stalagmites and other speleothems were also broken and arranged into various kinds of linear installations during somewhat later Pleistocene times, just as they had been in other European caves of the time (e.g.

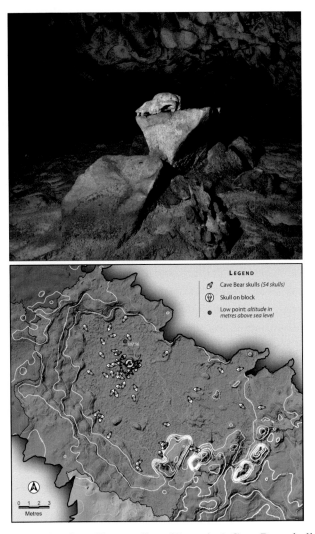

Figure 22 Skull Chamber, Chauvet Cave (France). A Cave Bear skull has been purposefully placed on a flat-top block fallen from the ceiling near the centre of the chamber. Fifty-four Cave Bear skulls encircle the block. Other kinds of Cave Bear bones are rare in this part of the cave (photo Jean-Jacques Delannoy; cartography by Julien Monney).

Arias Cabal et al. 2005) (Figures 23C and 23D). Speleothems are especially interesting for Quaternary researchers, for they can be dated by U-series dating, their thin laminations offering good chronological differentiation. Their accreted crystalline micro-layers are good sources of palaeo-environmental information, for they often retain trapped isotopic data, pollen and other micro-organisms

Figure 23 Examples of artificial installations made of broken stalagmites. (A) Circular structures at Bruniquel (France). (B), (C) Arrangement of stalagmites below a painted wall at La Garma (Spain). (D) Aligned broken stalagmites deep in the Cave of Saint Marcel d'Ardèche (France) (photo A by the Société Spéléo-Archéologique de Caussade; photos (B), (C) and (D) by Stéphane Jaillet).

that can act as proxies for palaeoclimates and biogeographic conditions (e.g. Couchoud et al. 2009; Drysdale et al. 2020; Green 2013; Kilhavn et al. 2022; Perrette et al. 2000, 2005; Quiers et al. 2015). The high-resolution study of their microscopically thin laminae makes it possible to reveal details of past environmental conditions at fine temporal scales rarely achievable with other kinds of data, such as seasonality. With this, details of contemporary human activities undertaken both inside and outside the site (such as soot from fires, trapped between a speleothem's accumulated laminae) can be cross-correlated (e.g. Vandevelde et al. 2017, 2018, 2020) (see Link 10, available as supplementary material at www.cambridge.org/mobilelandscapes). The ability to date speleothems by both radiocarbon and U-series dating only enhances the research potential of such sites and of the transformations that may have taken place there as a result of human occupation.

First described in 1995 with little fanfare (Rouzaud et al. 1995), the stalagmitic circles at Bruniquel have had major impacts on the scientific recognition of Neanderthal cognitive and social capabilities; the making of articulating circular structures deep in the cave imply coordinated social behaviour. So, too, does the lighting of fires for light and heat within the circle complex (Jaubert et al. 2016). More broadly, the findings have reminded archaeologists that broken speleothems, many of which had been bypassed by previous researchers at other caves, may in fact represent human-built structures and practices (for examples from La Garma and Chauvet Cave, see Ontañon 2003 and Delannoy et al. 2013, respectively).

This was the case for the Cave of Saint Marcel d'Ardèche in France, for example. Several thousand speleothems lie broken in its chambers, their breakage often previously assumed to have been caused by the large numbers of speleologists and tourists who had visited the cave after it opened to tourism in 1838. Recently though, some sectors of the cave have been subject to detailed archaeomorphological mapping. This has radically changed how the cave and the broken stalagmites are now understood. By mapping the position of each broken stalagmite on the floor, human-built structures have become apparent deep in the cave (Figure 24). Some seem to form pathways, others a step for the crossing of obstacles or to access parts of the cave that would otherwise be more difficult to reach. The cartographic work has helped refine the questions asked at the cave, and the research strategies, such as the identification of broken fragments of stalagmites with distal ends still present and through whose last growths can be dated by U-series dating, thereby giving maximum ages for when they had been broken and removed from their growing positions. U-series ages on the bases of stalagmites that subsequently began to grow on top of the anthropically constructed installations can also give minimum ages for when the installations were built (the constructions must be older than the stalagmites that later grew on top of them). Together, the two sets of ages frame the temporal window in which the installations must have been made. Initial results indicate that the stalagmitic installations are many thousands of years old, much earlier than the first speleological and tourism visits of the early nineteenth century (Jean-Jacques Delannoy, Jules Kemper and Stéphane Jaillet, unpublished data). These results raise new questions about the human past: the stalagmites were broken several kilometres deep into the cave, and required to travel down vertical passages that had long been thought unbreached and unbreachable prior to the era of modern cave exploration.

The question of architectural planning among societies of the deep past going back to the Last Glacial Maximum and beyond is also now broached at other sites such as La Garma (Spain), where, far from the cave's entrance, human groups cleared and delineated floor spaces with broken stalagmites during the Late Pleistocene (see Link 9, available as supplementary material at

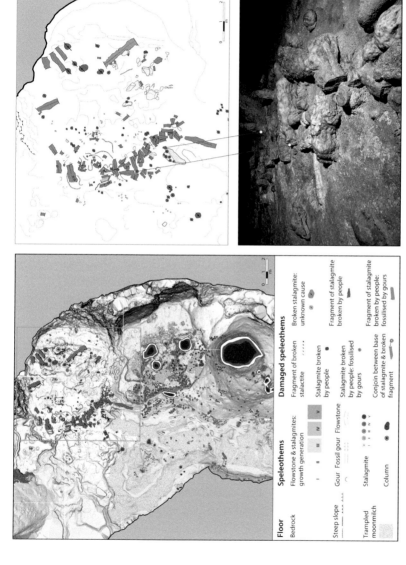

Figure 24 Archaeomorphological map of the Chamber of Columns, Cave of Saint Marcel d'Ardèche (France). The mapping of this part of the cave has brought to light 255 stalagmites whose bases remain in situ, and 453 broken fragments amidst the artificial structures currently under study. Most of the stalagmitic alignments, semi-circles and other structures making up the artificial installations are sealed below more recent flowstone and standing stalagmites, highlighting their great age beyond the period of nineteenth-century tourism (cartography by Jean-Jacques Delannoy, Jules Kemper and Stéphane Jaillet; photo by Jean-Jacques Delannoy).

Figure 25 Human skeleton of the Visigoth period (sixth to seventh century CE) surrounded by broken stalagmites in the cave of La Garma, Spain (photo by Bruno David).

www.cambridge.org/mobilelandscapes). Some 15,000 years later, Visigoths penetrated deep into the cave, and on its flat floor lay down a number of human bodies and, again, surrounded them with broken stalagmites. For reasons unknown, presumably ideological and probably religious, their skulls had been pulvarised to a pulp (Arias & Ontañón 2012; Arias Cabal et al. 2005; Gárate et al. 2011) (Figure 25). Again, the placement of stalagmites to delimit meaningful areas means that their purposeful arrangement can be dated, giving insights into the cave's social and cultural history.

4.3 Towards an Archaeology of Architectural Design

In archaeology the notion of architecture is generally associated with more or less centralised societies in urban settings – that is, with towns and cities. In Europe, archaeological interest in the notion of architecture largely begins with the Neolithic, both in relation to habitational structures and megalithic monuments. However, in recent years there has been serious questioning of the biases of such renditions, both conscious and unconscious (e.g. Urwin et al. 2022). Why is it that built structures of much greater time-depth are rarely discussed in terms of architectural design? It is as if the designers of such ancient structures are considered 'closer to nature' rather than sentient social beings capable of designing and building their own lived environments through culture. After all, by all lines of evidence, all peoples of the world have been fully modern *Homo sapiens*, both biologically and cognitively, for many tens of thousands of years. This problem of failure to represent human activities as fully modern applies also to very recent and contemporary peoples whose lifestyles differ(ed) from those of the West. Take as case in point the site of Borologa 1, in the Kimberley region of northern Australia. Here, in Kwini Aboriginal Country, rock outcrops were manually hollowed out with stone tools to make cavities. Hard quartzite rock was removed from a large monolith one layer at a time, extracted from the expanding cavity and repositioned outside. At this site alone, more than 3.5 tonnes of rock were removed, the ensuing alcoves' surfaces then painted (Delannoy et al. 2020b). Archaeology had completely missed these anthropic stone-working endeavours until archaeomorphological mapping revealed the source of each block of rock in the alcoves' outskirts.

But it is at the site of Nawarla Gabarnmang in Arnhem Land, in Jawoyn Country some 700 km east of Borologa in the central north of Australia, that archaeomorphological mapping really came into its own (e.g. Delannoy et al. 2013, 2017) (Figure 26). Here the concept of archaeomorphology, and archaeomorphological

Figure 26 Nawarla Gabarnmang (Arnhem Land, Australia). The double-ended rockshelter contains vast ceilings supported by c. 100 extant pillars. The pillars are separated by narrow corridors except for in some areas where pillars are missing, creating wide-open spaces. The ceiling reaches up to c. 2 m height across the site. The floor is covered with charcoal and ash from campfires (photo by Jean-Jacques Delannoy).

mapping, was coined and formalised, just as it was also already taking shape at Chauvet Cave on the other side of the world.

The history of Nawarla Gabarnmang's rock formation lies in its topography, the spatial structure of its rock matrix, the distribution of its detached rocks, the morphology of its rock surfaces and the accumulated sediments on its floor. Understanding that history requires combining all those lines of evidence into a single narrative incorporating the archaeology, geology, geomorphology and dating (Delannoy et al. 2017). Manual 2D mapping, 3D LiDAR modelling and excavation were the unifying tools.

The topography of the site immediately raises a number of questions: a large, double-ended rockshelter, Nawarla Gabarnmang has vast ceilings supported by c. 100 regularly spaced rock pillars (Figure 27). The rock matrix above the pillars is made of horizontal layers of quartzite that extend across the entire length and width of the site, except for at its lowermost layers – the ones that currently make up the ceiling – which are variably interrupted where large slabs have fallen down in some places. Here the ceiling is thus staggered. Those ceiling surfaces, along with many of the rock pillars, are now extensively painted with rock art.

Examining and mapping the painted ceiling brought to the fore a paradox: while the staggered ceiling testifies to the collapse of rock strata, their fallen rocks are missing from the floor below, except for a few small and isolated slabs of rock interspersed across the site. The eighteen archaeological excavations we undertook in various parts of the site were also largely devoid of buried rockfall. To investigate this conundrum, we mapped the floor and ceiling in great detail, treating the site as an interconnected three-dimensional space (rather than restricting the map to what is on the floor, as is often done in archaeology). It soon became apparent that where the horizontal distance between pillars was greatest – spanning up to 8 m from one pillar to the next in some cases – the archaeological traces of human presence in the form of paintings on the ceiling, and stone artefacts buried underground, for example, were most pronounced. Away from the open spaces, room closes rapidly as rock pillars abut each other, separated by very narrow corridors.

From these observations two possibilities emerged: (1) from the outset, the space between the pillars varied greatly, so that people had chosen to do things in those parts of the site where room between pillars was greatest; or (2) people had actively created the wider open spaces by knocking down pillars to make the extra room between the pillars that remained. To determine which was the correct alternative, the site's geology, geomorphology and archaeology were investigated. The petrography and geochemistry of each standing pillar and ceiling quartzite layer were characterised, so that the source of each block that remained on the floor could be determined. The processes of accumulation and

Figure 27 Floor and ceiling plans of Nawarla Gabarnmang (Arnhem Land, Australia). The floor plan shows the standing pillars, remnant pillar bases and

transport of soft sediments, as well as of rocks on the floor and in the excavated deposits, were investigated. The upper deposits were found to consist mainly of windblown sediments and remains of fireplaces, but their lower layers were mostly in situ decomposed bedrock. The contents of the archaeological excavations were closely inspected, including for whether each block that did lie buried possessed signs of flaking, along with whether they were associated with other kinds of cultural evidence such as charcoal from campfires, food remains, stone tools or ochre for painting. Some 200 radiocarbon dates on individual pieces of charcoal from the excavations gave a very detailed chronological picture of the floor sediments across the length and breadth of the site. A few dates on wasp nests and beeswax art on the ceiling gave minimum ages for the configuration of the current ceiling surfaces.

The combination of archaeomorphological mapping and excavation made it possible to identify which ceiling rock strata the blocks in and on the ground, within and immediately surrounding the rockshelter, had come from. What became clear was that the fallen slabs from the most recently collapsed ceiling strata were almost entirely absent from the floor and buried deposits. Furthermore, the floor and ceiling maps revealed that some 130 pillars were missing: the very upper strata of c. 50 of these were still attached to the ceiling (a few others only had their bases showing), but the pillars themselves were gone, as were their fallen blocks.

From these observations we then focused attention on the southwestern corner of the site where, unlike elsewhere in the rockshelter, tilted and partly dismantled pillars and numerous other large blocks were still present at ground level (Figure 28). Here a mudwasp nest on the ceiling was radiocarbon-dated to 11,510–11,940 cal BP (10,154 ± 40 BP, Wk-31730), signalling a minimum age for the extant ceiling on which it sits (Gunn 2018:608). Most of the blocks on

---

Caption for Figure 27 (cont.)

loose blocks, most of which were moved by people in the distant past.

The paucity of standing pillars at the centre of the site is evident, as is the abundance of evacuated blocks immediately beyond the northern and southern overhangs. The ceiling map, a mirror image of the floor with its own remnant traces, tells a similar story: remnant upper strata of missing pillars still adhere to the ceiling. The linear alignment of pillars and their intervening corridors also make it possible to identify where the missing pillars without remnant bases or ceiling strata once stood. The thicker pillar bases compared to their upper strata is a product of the distribution of mechanical stress (weight of the quatzite roof) (cartography by Jean-Jacques Delannoy).

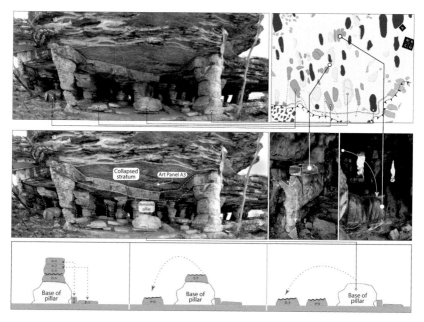

Figure 28 Archaeomorphological observations and interpretations of the southwest sector of Nawarla Gabarnmang. The morphogenic processes and sequence of human actions involved in the dismantling of pillars became evident through the mapping work (see the Figure 27 legend), and have been reverse-engineered in this figure. The *chaîne opératoire* followed during the dismantling of one of the pillars is shown in the various parts of this figure. The *modus operandi* was: (1) remove the upper parts of pillars; (2) collapse or directly dismantle each pillar one rock layer at a time; (3) the lower layer of the now-unsupported ceiling collapses; (4) rock art panel A3 is later painted. The petrography of the rock strata (here represented by strata D9 to D6) enables each dismantled and moved block to be sourced to its origininating layer in the rock matrix. In this southwestern sector of the site, the work of opening up the space remained unfinished, as is evident in the remnant pillar base and partially evacuated dismantled pillars. This is the last part of the site to have been opened up in this way. Scale: Squares A, C, G, K and N in the top-right of this figure are each 50 × 50 cm in area (photos and cartography by Jean-Jacques Delannoy).

the ground had come from the fallen pillars; the others came from the ceiling. However, and unlike elsewhere in the site, the ceiling blocks at ground level were not from the lowermost missing ceiling layers, but from the highest one (i.e. the last layer to have fallen). Only the very largest blocks, those that are too large to move, can be found at their drop-points. Those fallen blocks rest directly on the bases of missing pillars; the intervening fallen rock layers are

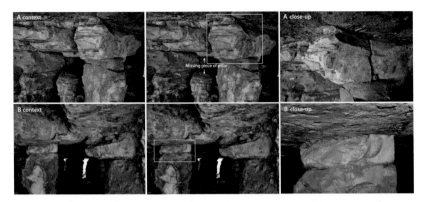

Figure 29 Two ways of removing the upper level of pillars prior to their toppling, southwest sector of Nawarla Gabarnmang. (A) Sectioning by flaking of stratum D0 at top of pillar. (B) Gradual removal by flaking away of stratum D-1 (photos by Bruno David).

missing. Many of the blocks on the ground contain the scars of impact blows, evidence that people had tried to flake them into smaller pieces. In many cases, block fragments could be conjoined back together again, even though they sometimes lay several metres apart: the partly fallen pillars and fallen ceiling strata had been dismantled, flaked apart and evacuated to the outer edges of the site. In some instances, the tops of still-standing pillars showed extensive flaking towards their removal (Figure 29). They represent the first steps in the dismantling of pillars: the removal of their upper layers creates a space that permits the pillars to be tilted, toppled and, once on the ground, dismantled layer by layer. The calibrated radiocarbon age on the ceiling indicates that these events took place more than 11,500 years ago. The reverse-engineering of the sequence of events that caused the pillars to disappear from the site ensued from a combination of archaeomorphological mapping, archaeological excavation, geomorphological observation and dating. The combination of archaeological and geomorphological observations, and in particular the site's detailed cartography, enabled a site-scale *chaîne opératoire* to be worked out for the opening up of the rockshelter.

At Nawarla Gabarnmang the extensively painted, wide-open ceilings evident today had been shaped by generations of stone workers and artists. At first the pillars were removed. Once removed, the ceiling lost its supports, causing layers of rock to fall down (whether or not those ceiling layers were also levered out or otherwise extracted by people is unknown). The fallen rock was then evacuated to the outer edges of the site, increasing the space between floor and ceiling in the process. Today the scree slopes fronting Nawarla Gabarnmang's northern and southern entrances contain hundreds, and possibly thousands, of amassed rock slabs that originated inside the shelter (Figure 30). The presence of a few isolated and sometimes flaked rock slabs in the excavations indicates that this process of rock working and evacuation began sometime between 35,000 cal BP and 23,000 cal BP and continued until c. 11,500 cal BP, after which it stopped (but the painting continued) (David et al. 2017; Delannoy et al. 2017, 2018) (Figure 31). The architectural shaping of Nawarla Gabarnmang into the site we see today took place over a thousand generations of stone workers and, both during this time and later, artists.

The transdisciplinary, archaeomorphological reading of Nawarla Gabarnmang's deep-time history from a 'building perspective' has not only shed new light on the site as an enduring node in the landscape, one that was visited many times over tens of thousands of years, but also on the possibility that other sites may not be quite what they seem at first glance. While Nawarla Gabarnmang may be an extraordinary site, many others have since been recognised to also feature such traces of the human hand, such as at Borologa in the Kimberley (Delannoy et al. 2020b). But one does not have to be faced with an extensively shaped rockshelter to make the point: many, and perhaps most, caves and rockshelters that have witnessed the presence of people have been modified in one way or another, be it in their hollowing out such as at Nawarala Gabarnmang and Borologa 1 in Jawoyn Country and Kwini Country in northern Australia, respectively, or in the moving of individual blocks to make steps, such as at Cloggs Cave in GunaiKurnai Country in southeastern

Figure 30 Evacuated blocks at the southern (bottom-left photo) and northern (bottom-right photo) entrances of Nawarla Gabarnmang (photos and 3D model by Jean-Jacques Delannoy).

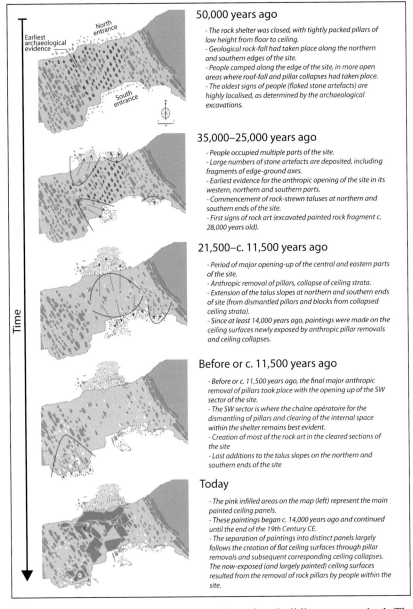

50,000 years ago

- *The rock shelter was closed, with tightly packed pillars of low height from floor to ceiling.*
- *Geological rock-fall had taken place along the northern and southern edges of the site.*
- *People camped along the edge of the site, in more open areas where roof-fall and pillar collapses had taken place.*
- *The oldest signs of people (flaked stone artefacts) are highly localised, as determined by the archaeological excavations.*

35,000–25,000 years ago

- *People occupied multiple parts of the site.*
- *Large numbers of stone artefacts are deposited, including fragments of edge-ground axes.*
- *Earliest evidence for the anthropic opening of the site in its western, northern and southern parts.*
- *Commencement of rock-strewn taluses at northern and southern ends of the site.*
- *First signs of rock art (excavated painted rock fragment c. 28,000 years old).*

21,500–c. 11,500 years ago

- *Period of major opening-up of the central and eastern parts of the site.*
- *Anthropic removal of pillars, collapse of ceiling strata.*
- *Extension of the talus slopes at northern and southern ends of site (from dismantled pillars and blocks from collapsed ceiling strata).*
- *Since at least 14,000 years ago, paintings were made on the ceiling surfaces newly exposed by anthropic pillar removals and ceiling collapses.*

Before or c. 11,500 years ago

- *Before or c. 11,500 years ago, the final major anthropic removal of pillars took place with the opening up of the SW sector of the site.*
- *The SW sector is where the chaîne opératoire for the dismantling of pillars and clearing of the internal space within the shelter remains best evident.*
- *Creation of most of the rock art in the cleared sections of the site*
- *Last additions to the talus slopes on the northern and southern ends of the site*

Today

- *The pink infilled areas on the map (left) represent the main painted ceiling panels.*
- *These paintings began c. 14,000 years ago and continued until the end of the 19th Century CE.*
- *The separation of paintings into distinct panels largely follows the creation of flat ceiling surfaces through pillar removals and subsequent corresponding ceiling collapses. The now-exposed (and largely painted) ceiling surfaces resulted from the removal of rock pillars by people within the site.*

Figure 31 Nawarla Gabarnmang as seen through a 'building perspective'. The chronological phases are based on a combination of geomorphological and archaeological evidence, as dated by some 200 radiocarbon dates and cross-correlated in the cartographic work. Nawarla Gabarnmang owes its current morphology to a thousand generations of stone workers over a period of c. 25,000 years (cartography by Jean-Jacques Delannoy).

Australia (Delannoy et al. 2020a). For some sites, Indigenous knowledge holders may retain details of those cultural events, but at others this may not be so, as in the case of Nawarla Gabarnmang and Borologa 1, which both stretch back to the Pleistocene–Holocene boundary and beyond. In those cases, we would usually not know that the sites are themselves shaped artefacts of massive scale, until the coordinated cartographic work incorporating multiple strands of evidence was done.

4.4 Further Readings

David, B., Urwin, C., Fresløv, J., Mullett, R. & Phillips, C. (2023). Engaging and designing place: Furnishings and the architecture of archaeological sites in Aboriginal Australia. In McNiven, I. J. & David, B. (Eds.), *The Oxford Handbook of the Archaeology of Indigenous Australia and New Guinea*, pp. 473–94. Oxford: Oxford University Press.

Delannoy, J.-J., David, B., Geneste, J.-M., et al. (2013). The social construction of caves and rockshelters: Chauvet Cave (France) and Nawarla Gabarnmang (Australia). *Antiquity* 87(335):12–29. https://doi.org/10.1017/S0003598X00048596.

Delannoy, J.-J., David, B., Geneste, J.-M., et al. (2017). Engineers of the Arnhem Land plateau: Evidence for the origins and transformation of sheltered spaces at Nawarla Gabarnmang. In David, B., Taçon, P. S. C., Delannoy, J.-J. & Geneste, J.-M. (Eds.), *The Archaeology of Rock Art in Western Arnhem Land, Australia*, pp. 197–243. Terra Australis 47. Canberra: ANU Press. https://press-files.anu.edu.au/downloads/press/n3991/pdf/ch10.pdf.

Delannoy, J.-J. & Geneste, J.-M. (Eds.) (2020). *Monographie de la Grotte Chauvet-Pont d'Arc: Volume 1 – Atlas de la Grotte Chauvet-Pont d'Arc*. Paris: Documents de l'Archéologie Française, Éditions de la Maison des Sciences de l'Homme.

Genuite, K., Delannoy, J.-J., Bahain, J.-J., et al. (2021). Dating the landscape evolution around the Chauvet-Pont d'Arc cave. *Scientific Reports* 11:8944. https://doi.org/10.1038/s41598-021-88240-5.

Jaubert, J., Verheyden, S., Genty,D., et al. (2016). Early Neanderthal constructions deep in Bruniquel Cave in southwestern France. *Nature* 534:111–4. https://doi.org/10.1038/nature18291.

Lock, G. (Ed.) (2000). *Beyond the Map: Archaeology and Spatial Technologies*. Amsterdam: IOS Press.

McFadyen, L. (2008). Building and architecture as landscape practice. In David, B. & Thomas, J. (Eds.), *Handbook of Landscape Archaeology*, pp. 307–14. Walnut Creek: Left Coast Press.

Montelle, Y.-P. (2022). The skull chamber in the Chauvet Cave: En route towards a theatre. *TDR: The Drama Review* 66(2):10–26. https://muse.jhu .edu/article/858113N1.

Ontañón, R. (2003). Sols et structures d'habitat du Paléolithique supérieur, nouvelles données depuis les Cantabres: La Galerie Inférieure de La Garma (Cantabria, Espagne). *L'Anthropologie* 107(3):333–63. https://doi.org/ 10.1016/S0003-5521(03)00037-2.

Vandevelde, S., Brochier, J. É., Desachy, B., Petit, C. & Slimak, L. (2018). Sooted concretions: A new micro-chronological tool for high temporal resolution archaeology. *Quaternary International* 474(Part B): 103–18. https://doi .org/10.1016/j.quaint.2017.10.031.

5 Conclusion

In this Element, we have presented examples of how the deep-time history of cultural landscapes and their enduring sites can be examined archaeologically. In doing so, we have highlighted five key points:

1. That at its core the archaeology of sites and landscapes is also an archaeology of mobility and temporality, of moving and doing things across space and through time (Section 2).
2. That when trying to understand what people did in the past, it is important to contextualise the individual sites of past activities in their broader landscapes. This will often require understanding and reconstructing what the environment of a site was like for the period in question (Section 3).
3. That doing landscape archaeology requires positioning archaeological materials, whether they be artefacts, assemblages, sites or sets of sites, in space and time; it is about doing *spatial history* (Section 4).
4. In landscape reconstructions, *the details matter*. A site and its broader landscape are, and can be researched as, artefacts in their own right. The physical traces of the past can be studied as *chaînes opératoires* of those sites' unfolding constructions. This is best achieved through an integrated, transdisciplinary approach.
5. Using the broad span of methods and approaches at our disposal, archaeology and its kin disciplines can work out precisely how each place was built, when and where.

Each of these themes brings to the fore two key points. The first is that when asking archaeological questions about a place, it is more useful to ask how it has been *engaged* as a node in a landscape, rather than ask whether it is 'natural' or 'cultural'. Determining what happened in the past, how and when requires not just a focus on the particular site under investigation but also a readiness to shift the spatial focus so that the object of study can be positioned in its broader landscape setting. Landscape archaeology often requires the researcher to repeatedly adjust their gaze, and their enquiries, from one analytical scale to another, and this scalar shift needs to be integrated as a conceptual and methodological practice. Understanding a localised place requires positioning it in its broader landscape setting, rich in time and mobility, keeping in mind all that the notion of landscape implies.

The second key point, and it is one that has probably become obvious by now, is that the notion of 'cultural landscape' is a tautology, for landscapes are *always* cultural. From the very moment of its inhabitation, a landscape is already culturally conceived as *meaningful* in one way or another. Doing an archaeology of 'cultural landscapes' is doubly so, in that it is about trying to envisage how people were situated in meaningful places in the past, and how that situatedness of material engagements is inherently social (because places are socially positioned). In archaeology, that meaningful situatedness becomes accessible through the things that people left behind, as they engaged with each other in their worlds.

References

Albarella, U. & Serjeantson, D. (2002). A passion for pork: Butchery and cooking at the British Neolithic site of Durrington Walls. In Miracle, P. T. & Milner, M. (Eds.), *Consuming Passions and Patterns of Consumption*, pp. 33–49. Cambridge: MacDonald Institute.

Aldred, O. (2020). *The Archaeology of Movement*. Milton: Taylor & Francis Group.

Antonioli, F. (2012). Sea level change in western-central Mediterranean since 300 kyr: Comparing global sea level curves with observed data. *Alpine and Mediterranean Quaternary* 25(1):15–23. https://amq.aiqua.it/index.php/amq/article/view/41.

Arfib, B. (2021). A l'origine de la grotte Cosquer, le karst des Calanques. In Vanrell, L. & Olive, M. (Eds.), *La Grotte Cosquer:Trente Ans de Recherches. Dossiers d'Archéologie* 408:20–5.

Arias, P. & Ontañón, R. (2012). La Garma (Spain): Long-term human activity in a karst system. In Bergsvik, K. N. & Skeates, R. (Eds.), *Caves in Context: The Cultural Significance of Caves and Rockshelters in Europe*, pp. 101–17. Oxford: Oxbow Books. https://doi.org/10.2307/j.ctvh1djk4.12.

Arias, P. & Ontañon, R. (2014). La Garma: Un proyecto orientado al estudio del arte paleolítico, su contexto y su conservación. In Corchón, M. S. & Menéndez, M. (Eds.), *Cien Años de Arte Rupestre Paleolítico*, pp. 173–94. Salamanca: Ediciones Universidad de Salamanca.

Arias Cabal, P., Ontañon Peredo, R., Álbares Fernández, E., et al. (2005). La estructura Magdaleniense de La Garma A: Aproximación a la organización espacial de un hábitat paleolítico. In Ferreira Bicho, N. & Corchón Rodriguez, M. S. (Eds.), *O Paleolítico: Actas do IV Congresso de Arqueologia Peninsular (Faro, 14 a 19 Setembro de 2004)*, pp. 123–42. Faro: Centro de Estudos de Património, Universidade do Algarve.

Ascher, R. (1962). Ethnography for archaeology: A case from the Seri Indians. *Ethnology* 1:360–9. https://doi.org/10.2307/3772948.

Ascher, R. (1961). Analogy in archaeological interpretation. *Southwestern Journal of Anthropology* 17:317–25. https://doi.org/10.1086/soutjanth.17.4.3628943.

Bailey, G. (1981). Concepts, timescales and explanations in economic prehistory. In Sheridan, A. & Bailey, G. (Eds.), *Economic Archaeology*, pp. 97–117. Oxford: British Archaeological Reports.

Bailey, G. (1983). Concepts of time in Quaternary prehistory. *Annual Review of Anthropology* 12:165–92. https://doi.org/10.1146/annurev.an.12.100183.001121.

Bailey, G. & Galanidou, N. (2009). Caves, palimpsests and dwelling spaces: Examples from the Upper Palaeolithic of south-east Europe. *World Archaeology* 41(2):215–41. https://doi.org/10.1080/00438240902843733.

Bard, E. & Lambeck, K. (2000). Sea-level change along the French Mediterranean coast for the past 30,000 years. *Earth and Planetary Science Letters* 175:203–22.

Barker, G. (1995). *A Mediterranean Valley: Landscape Archaeology and Annales History in the Biferno Valley.* London: Leicester University Press.

Basso, K. (1996). *Wisdom Sits in Places: Landscape and Language Among the Western Apache.* Albuquerque: University of New Mexico Press.

Bender, B. (2002). Time and landscape. *Current Anthropology* 43(Supplement): S10–S112. https://doi.org/10.1086/339561.

Bernstein, R. J. (1983). *Beyond Objectivism and Relativism: Science, Hermeneutics, and Praxis.* Philadelphia: University of Pennsylvania Press.

Binford, L. R. (1973). Interassemblage variability – The Mousterian and the 'functional' argument. In Renfrew, C. (Ed.), *The Explanation of Culture Change*, pp. 227–54. London: Duckworth.

Binford, L. R. (1978). *Nunamiut Ethnoarchaeology.* New York: Academic Press.

Binford, L. R. (1980). Willow smoke and dog's tails: Hunter-gatherer settlement systems and archaeological site formation. *American Antiquity* 45:4–20. https://doi.org/10.2307/279653.

Binford, L. R. (1981). Behavioral archaeology and the 'Pompeii premise'. *Journal of Anthropological Research* 37(3):195–208. https://doi.org/10.1086/jar.37.3.3629723.

Binford, L. R. (1982). The archaeology of place. *Journal of Anthropological Archaeology* 1(1):5–31. https://doi.org/10.1016/0278-4165(82)90006-X.

Binford, L. & Binford, S. (1966). A preliminary analysis of functional variability in the Mousterian of the Levallois facies. *American Anthropologist* 68:238–95. www.jstor.org/stable/670742.

Bintliff, J. L. (1997). Catastrophe, chaos and complexity: The death, decay and rebirth of towns from antiquity to today. *Journal of European Archaeology* 5:67–90. https://doi.org/10.1179/096576697800660302.

Bintliff, J. L. (1991). The contribution of an Annaliste/structural history approach to archaeology. In Bintliff, J. L. (Ed.), *The Annales School and Archaeology*, pp. 1–33. Leicester: Leicester University Press.

Bishop, M. C. (2014). *The Secret History of the Roman Roads of Britain: And Their Impact on Military History.* Barnsley: Pen and Sword.

Blair, S. (2010). Missing the boat in lithic procurement: Watercraft and the bulk procurement of tool-stone on the Maritime Peninsula. *Journal of*

Anthropological Archaeology 29:33–46. https://doi.org/10.1016/j.jaa.2009 .10.006.

Bordes, F. (1953). Essaie de classification des industries 'moustériennes'. *Bulletin de la Société Préhistorique Française* 50:457–66. www.jstor.org/ stable/27914848.

Bordes, F. (1973). On the chronology and contemporaneity of different Palaeolithic cultures in France. In Renfrew, C. (Ed.), *The Explanation of Culture Change*, pp. 217–26. London: Duckworth.

Bowen, G. J. (2010). Isoscapes: Spatial pattern in isotopic biogeochemistry. *Annual Review of Earth and Planetary Sciences* 38:161–87. https://doi.org/ 10.1146/annurev-earth-040809-152429.

Braudel, F. (1972 [1949]). *The Mediterranean and the Mediterranean World in the Age of Philip II*. New York: Harper & Row.

Burke, A. (2015). Visuo-spatial integration and spatial cognition: A comment on Bruner & Lozano. (2014). *Journal of Anthropological Sciences* 93:177–80.

Casey, E. S. (1993). *Getting Back into Place: Toward a Renewed Understanding of the Place-World*. Bloomington: Indiana University Press.

Casey, E. S. (1996). How to get from space to place in a fairly short stretch of time: Phenomenological prolegomena. In Feld, S. & Basso, K. H. (Eds.), *Senses of Place*, pp. 13–52. Santa Fe: School of American Research Press.

Casey, E. S. (1997). *The Fate of Place: A Philosophical History*. Berkeley: University of California Press.

Casey, E. S. (2001). Between geography and philosophy: What does it mean to be in the place-world? *Annals of the Association of American Geographers* 91(4):683–93. www.jstor.org/stable/3651229.

Cherry, J. F. (1982). A preliminary definition of site distribution on Melos. In Renfrew, C. & Wagstaff, M. (Eds.), *An Island Polity: The Archaeology of Exploitation in Melos*, pp. 10–23. Cambridge: Cambridge University Press.

Cherry, J. F. (1983). Frogs around the pond: Perspectives on current archaeological survey projects in the Mediterranean region. In Keller, R. & Rupp, D. W. (Eds.), *Archaeological Survey in the Mediterranean Area*, pp. 375–416. Oxford: British Archaeological Reports.

Cherry, J. F., Davis. J. L. & Mantzourani, E. (1991). *Landscape Archaeology as Long-Term History: Northern Keos in the Cycladic Islands*. Los Angeles: Institute of Archaeology.

Childe, V. G. (1950). *Prehistoric Migrations in Europe*. Serie A, Volume 20. Oslo: Instituttet for *Sammenlignende Kulturforskning*.

Childe, V. G. (1958). *The Prehistory of European Society*. London: Penguin.

Cita, M. B. (1982). The Messinian salinity crisis in the Mediterranean: A review. *Alpine-Mediterranean Geodynamics* 7:113–40. https://doi.org/10.1029/GD007p0113.

Clarke, D. (1972). *Models in Archaeology*. London: Duckworth.

Clauzon, G., Suc, J. P., Gautier, F., Berger, A. & Loutre, M. F. (1996). Alternate interpretation of the Messinian salinity crisis: Controversy resolved? *Geology* 24(4):363–6. https://doi.org/10.1130/0091-7613(1996)024<0363:AIOTMS>2.3.CO;2.

Clottes, J. (1996). Thematic changes in Upper Palaeolithic art: A view from the Grotte Chauvet. *Antiquity* 70(268):276–88. https://doi.org/10.1017/S0003598X00083277.

Clottes, J. (2018). European Palaeolithic rock art and spatial structures. In David, B. & McNiven, I. J. (Eds.), *The Oxford Handbook of the Archaeology and Anthropology of Rock Art*, pp. 397–409. Oxford: Oxford University Press. https://doi.org/10.1093/oxfordhb/9780190607357.013.6.

Clottes, J., Beltrán, A., Courtin, J. & Cosquer, H. (1992). The Cosquer Cave on Cape Morgiou, Marseilles. *Antiquity* 66(252):583–98. https://doi.org/10.1017/S0003598X00039314.

Clottes, J., Courtin, J. & Vanrell, L. (2005). *Cosquer Redécouvert*. Paris: Seuil.

Collina-Girard, J. (1996). Préhistoire et karst littoral: La grotte Cosquer et les calanques marseillaises. *Karstologia* 27:27–40. www.persee.fr/doc/karst_0751-7688_1996_num_27_1_2363.

Collina-Girard, J. (2014). Karst memories above and beneath the sea: Marseilles and its continental shelf during the Cosquer Cave occupation. In Fort, M. & André, M.-F. (Eds.), *Landscapes and Landforms of France*, pp. 229–39. Dordrecht: Springer.

Collinard-Girard, J. & Arfib, B. (2010). Le karst polyphasé des Calanques et la grotte Coquer. In Audra, P. (Ed.), *Grottes et Karsts de France. Karstologia Mémoires* 19:242–243. https://halshs.archives-ouvertes.fr/halshs-00505480.

Conkey, M. W. (1980). The identification of prehistoric hunter-gatherer aggregation site: The case of Altamira. *Current Anthropology* 21(5):609–30. https://doi.org/10.1086/202540.

Couchoud, I., Genty, D., Hoffmann, D., Drysdale, R. & Blamart, D. (2009). Millennial-scale climate variability during the Last Interglacial recorded in a speleothem from south-western France. *Quaternary Science Reviews* 28 (27–28):3263–74. https://doi.org/10.1016/j.quascirev.2009.08.014.

Craig, O. E., Shillito, L. M., Albarella, U., et al. (2015). Feeding Stonehenge: Cuisine and consumption at the Late Neolithic site of Durrington Walls. *Antiquity* 89(347):1096–109. https://doi.org/10.15184/aqy.2015.110.

Crawford, O. G. S. (1953). *Archaeology in the Field*. London: Phoenix House.

Crellin, R. J. (2020). *Change and Archaeology*. London: Routledge.

Crellin, R. J. & Harris, O. J. (2020). Beyond binaries: Interrogating ancient DNA. *Archaeological Dialogues* 27(1):37–56. https://doi.org/10.1017/S1380203820000082.

Cribb, R. (2004). *Nomads in Archaeology*. Cambridge: Cambridge University Press.

David, B., Arnold, L. J., Delannoy, J.-J., et al. (2021c). Late survival of megafauna refuted for Cloggs Cave, SE Australia: Implications for the Australian Late Pleistocene megafauna extinction debate. *Quaternary Science Reviews* 253:106781. https://doi.org/10.1016/j.quascirev.2020.106781.

David, B., Delannoy, J.-J., Gunn, R. G., et al. (2017). Dating painted Panel E1 at Nawarla Gabarnmang, southern Arnhem Land plateau. In David. B., Taçon, P. S. C., Delannoy, J.-J. & Geneste, J.-M. (Eds.), *The Archaeology of Rock Art in Western Arnhem Land, Australia*, pp. 245–301. Terra Australis 47. Canberra: ANU Press. https://press-files.anu.edu.au/downloads/press/n3991/pdf/ch11.pdf.

David, B., Delannoy, J.-J., Katherine, M., Whear, R., Geneste, J.-M. & Gollings, J. (2018). Nawarla Gabarnmang: A spectacular rock-shelter in Arnhem Land, in Australia's far north, questions assumptions about the nature of design, provoking reflection on the boundaries between the natural and the built. *Landscape Architecture Australia* 158:52–58. https://landscapeaustralia.com/articles/nawarla-gabarnmang/.

David, B., Fresløv, J., Mullett, R., et al. (2021a). Paradigm shifts and ontological turns at Cloggs cave, GunaiKurnai Country, Australia. In Moro Abadía, O. & Porr, M. (Eds.),*Ontologies of Rock Art: Images, Relational Approaches, and Indigenous Knowledges*, pp. 135–60. London: Routledge.

David, B., Fresløv, J., Mullett, R., et al. (2021b). 50 years and worlds apart: Rethinking the Early Holocene abandonment of Cloggs Cave (East Gippsland, SE Australia) five decades after its initial archaeological excavation and in light of GunaiKurnai world views. *Australian Archaeology* 87(1):1–20.

David, B., Taçon, P., Delannoy, J.-J. & Geneste, J.-M. (Eds.) (2017). *The Archaeology of Rock Art in Western Arnhem Land, Australia*. Terra Australis 47. Canberra: ANU Press. http://doi.org/10.22459/TA47.11.2017.

Debard, E., Delannoy, J.-J., Ferrier, C., et al. (2020). Salle des Bauges (partie sud). In Delannoy, J.-J. & Geneste, J.-M. (Eds.), *Monographie de la Grotte Chauvet-Pont d'Arc: Volume 1 – Atlas de la Grotte Chauvet-Pont d'Arc*, pp. 206–11. Paris: Documents de l'Archéologie Française, Éditions de la Maison des Sciences de l'Homme.

de Champlain, S. (1613). *Les Voyages du Sieur de Champlain Xaintongeois, Capitaine Ordinaire Pour le Roy en la Marine*. Paris: Iean Berjon.

Deal, M. (2002). Aboriginal land and resource use in New Brunswick during the late prehistoric and early contact periods. In Hart, J. P. & Reith, C. B. (Eds.), *Northeast Subsistence-Settlement Change A.D. 700–1300*, pp. 321–44. New York State Museum Bulletin 496. Albany: New York State Education Department.

Delannoy, J.-J. (2018). Le Karst souterrain et ses temporalité: Vecteurs de dialogues interdisciplinaires – Discussions autour des notions d'instants, d'archives, de mémoires et d'indicateurs. *Karstologia Mémoires* 20:31–51. https://hal.archives-ouvertes.fr/hal-01895749/.

Delannoy, J.-J., Berthet, J., Stouvenot, C. & Monney, J. (2022). Morphogenèse des espaces ornés de plein-air en milieu tropical humide: Analyse archéo-géomorphologique des sites d'art rupestre précolombiens de Trois Rivières (Guadeloupe, Petites Antilles). *Géomorphologie: Relief, Processus, Environnement* 28(1):33–51. https://doi.org/10.4000/geomorphologie .16561.

Delannoy, J.-J., David, B., Fresløv, J., et al. (2020a). Geomorphological context and formation history of Cloggs Cave: What was the cave like when people inhabited it? *Journal of Archaeological Science: Reports* 33:102461. https:// doi.org/10.1016/j.jasrep.2020.102461.

Delannoy, J.-J., David, B., Geneste, J.-M., et al. (2013). The social construction of caves and rockshelters: Chauvet Cave (France) and Nawarla Gabarnmang (Australia). *Antiquity* 87(335):12–29. https://doi.org/10.1017/S0003598X000 48596.

Delannoy, J.-J., David, B., Geneste, J.-M., Katherine, M., Sadier, B. & Gunn, R. (2017). Engineers of the Arnhem Land plateau: Evidence for the origins and transformation of sheltered spaces at Nawarla Gabarnmang. In David, B., Taçon, P. S. C., Delannoy, J.-J. & Geneste, J.-M. (Eds.), *The Archaeology of Rock Art in Western Arnhem Land, Australia*, pp. 197–243. Terra Australis 47. Canberra: ANU Press. https://press-files.anu.edu.au/downloads/press/ n3991/pdf/ch10.pdf.

Delannoy, J.-J., David, B., Genuite, K., et al. (2020b). Investigating the anthropic construction of rock art sites through archaeomorphology: The case of Borologa, Kimberley, Australia. *Journal of Archaeological Method and Theory* 27(3):631–69. https://doi.org/10.1007/s10816-020-09477-4.

Delannoy, J.-J., David, B., Gunn, R. G., Geneste, J.-M. & Jaillet, S. (2018). Archaeomorphological mapping: Rock art and the architecture of place. In David, B. & McNiven, I. J. (Eds.),*The Oxford Handbook of the Archaeology and Anthropology of Rock Art*, pp. 833–56. Oxford: Oxford University Press. https://doi.org/10.1093/oxfordhb/9780190607357.013.46.

Delannoy, J.-J., Debard, E., Ferrier, C., Kervazo, B. & Perrette, Y. (2001). La cartographie morphologique souterraine: Apports aux reconstitutions paléogéographiques et paléoenvironnementales – Application à la grotte Chauvet (Ardèche – France). *Quaternaire* 12(4):235–48.

Delannoy, J.-J. & Geneste, J.-M. (Eds.) (2020). *Monographie de la Grotte Chauvet-Pont d'Arc: Volume 1 – Atlas de la Grotte Chauvet-Pont d'Arc.* Paris: Documents de l'Archéologie Française, Éditions de la Maison des Sciences de l'Homme.

Delannoy, J.-J., Sadier, B., Jaillet, S., Ployon, E. & Geneste, J.-M. (2010). Reconstitution de l'entrée préhistorique de la grotte Chauvet-Pont d'Arc (Ardèche, France): Les apports de l'analyse géomorphologique et de la modélisation 3D. *Karstologia* 56:17–34. www.persee.fr/doc/karst_0751-7688_2010_num_56_1_2679.

D'Ericco, F. (1994). Birds of the Grotte Cosquer: The Great Auk and Palaeolithic prehistory. *Antiquity* 68(258):39–47. https://doi.org/10.1017/S0003598X00046172.

Drysdale, R., Couchoud, I., Zanchetta, G., et al. (2020). Magnesium in sub-aqueous speleothems as a potential palaeotemperature proxy. *Nature Communications* 11:5027. https://doi.org/10.1038/s41467-020-18083-7.

Eisenmann, S., Bánffy, E., van Dommelen, P., et al. (2018). Reconciling material cultures in archaeology with genetic data: The nomenclature of clusters emerging from archaeogenomic analysis. *Scientific Reports* 8(13003):1–12. https://doi.org/10.1038/s41598-018-31123-z.

Evans, A. M., Flatman, J. C. & Flemming, N. C. (Eds.) (2014). *Prehistoric Archaeology on the Continental Shelf: A Global Review.* New York: Springer.

Evans, J., Mee, K., Chenery, C. A., Lee, K. A. & Marchant, A. P. (2018). User guide for the biosphere (version 1) dataset and web portal. *British Geological Survey Open Report*, OR/18/005. www.bgs.ac.uk/datasets/biosphere-isotope-domains-gb/.

Evans, J., Pearson, M. P., Madgwick, R., Sloane, H. & Albarella, U. (2019). Strontium and oxygen isotope evidence for the origin and movement of cattle at Late Neolithic Durrington Walls, UK. *Archaeological and Anthropological Sciences* 11(10):5181–97. https://doi.org/10.1007/s12520-019-00849-w.

Feld, S. & Basso, K. H. (Eds.) (1996). *Senses of Place.* Santa Fe: School for Advanced Research.

Felding, L. (2016). The Egtved Girl: Travel, trade & alliances in the Bronze Age. *Adoranten* 2015:5–20.

Fisher, G. (1965). Report on the Indian camp site locations on the Reversing Falls portage with reference to archaeological excavations in the area from 1954–1964. Unpublished manuscript on file at the New Brunswick Museum, Saint John.

Fox, C. (1923). *The Archaeology of the Cambridge Region: A Topographical Study of the Bronze, Early Iron, Roman and Anglo-Saxon Ages, with an Introductory Note on the Neolithic Age*. Cambridge: Cambridge University Press.

Frachetti, M. D. (2011). Migration concepts in central Eurasian archaeology. *Annual Review of Anthropology* 40:195–212. https://doi.org/10.1146/annurev-anthro-081309-145939.

Frei, K. M. & Price, D. T. (2012). Strontium isotopes and human mobility in prehistoric Denmark. *Archaeological and Anthropological Science* 4(2): 103–14. https://doi.org/10.1007/s12520-011-0087-7.

Frei, K. M., Mannering, U., Kristiansen, K., et al. (2015). Tracing the dynamic life story of a Bronze Age female. *Scientific Reports* 5(1):1–7. https://doi.org/10.1038/srep10431.

Frei, K. M., Villa, C., Jørkov, M. L., et al. (2017). A matter of months: High precision migration chronology of a Bronze Age female. *PLoS ONE* 12(6): e0178834. https://doi.org/10.1371/journal.pone.0178834.

Frei, R., Frank A. B. & Frei, K. M. (2022). The proper choice of proxies for relevant strontium isotope baselines used for provenance and mobility studies in glaciated terranes – Important messages from Denmark. *Science of the Total Environment* 821(153394):1–13. https://doi.org/10.1016/j.scitotenv.2022.153394.

Frieman, C. J. & Hofmann, D. (2019). Present pasts in the archaeology of genetics, identity, and migration in Europe: A critical essay. *World Archaeology* 51(4): 528–45. https://doi.org/10.1080/00438243.2019.1627907.

Furholt, M. (2018). Massive migrations? The impact of recent aDNA studies on our view of third millennium Europe. *European Journal of Archaeology* 21(2):159–91. https://doi.org/10.1017/eaa.2017.43.

Ganong, W. F. (1899). *A Monograph of Historic Sites in the Province of New Brunswick*. Ottawa: J. Hope.

Gárate, J. A. H. (2011). La utilización sepulcral de las cuevas en época visigoda: Los casos de Las Penas, La Garma y El Portillo del Arenal (Cantabria). *Munibe Antropologia-Arkeologia* 62:351–402.

Genty, D., Blamart, D., Dewilde, F., et al. (2020). Datation U/Th des spéléothèmes. In Delannoy, J.-J. & Geneste, J.-M. (Eds.), *Monographie de la Grotte Chauvet-Pont d'Arc: Volume 1 – Atlas de la Grotte Chauvet-Pont d'Arc*, pp. 126–9. Paris: Documents de l'Archéologie Française, Éditions de la Maison des Sciences de l'Homme.

Genuite, K., Delannoy, J.-J., Bahain, J.-J., et al. (2021). Dating the landscape evolution around the Chauvet-Pont d'Arc cave. *Scientific Reports* 11:8944. https://doi.org/10.1038/s41598-021-88240-5.

Genuite, K., Delannoy, J.-J., David, B., et al. (2021). Determining the origin and changing shape of landscape-scale rock formations with three-dimensional modelling: The Borologa rock shelters, Kimberley region, Australia. *Geoarchaeology* 36(4):662–80. https://doi.org/10.1002/gea.21863.

Gesner, A. (1842). *Fourth Report on the Geological Survey of the Province of New Brunswick.* Saint John NB: Henry Chubb.

Gibson, C. D. (2021). Making journeys, blurring boundaries and celebrating transience: A movement toward archaeologies of in-betweenness. In Gibson, C. D., Frieman, C. & Cleary, K. (Eds.), *Making Journeys: Archaeologies of Movement*, pp. 1–15. Oxford: Oxbow Books.

Green, H. (2013). Exploring the palaeoclimate potential of south east Australian speleothems. Unpublished PhD thesis, The University of Melbourne, Melbourne. http://hdl.handle.net/11343/39765.

Green, H., Gleadow, A., Finch, D., Myers, C. & McGovern, J. (2021). Micro-stromatolitic laminations and the origins of engraved, oxalate-rich accretions from Australian rock art shelters. *Geoarchaeology* 36(6):964–77. https://doi.org/10.1002/gea.21882.

Gunn, R. (2018). *Art of the Ancestors: Spatial and Temporal Patterning in the Ceiling Rock Art of Nawarla Gabarnmang, Arnhem Land, Australia.* Oxford: Archaeopress.

Haak, W., Lazaridis, I., Patterson, N., et al. (2015). Massive migration from the steppe was a source for Indo-European languages in Europe. *Nature* 522 (7555):207–11. https://doi.org/10.1038/nature14317.

Hacıgüzeller, P. (2020). Applications of correlation and linear regression. In Gillings, M., Hacıgüzeller, P. & Lock, G. (Eds.), *Archaeological Spatial Analysis: A Methodological Guide*, pp. 135–54. New York: Routledge.

Hakenbeck, S. E. (2019). Genetics, archaeology and the far right: An unholy Trinity. *World Archaeology* 51(4):517–27. https://doi.org/10.1080/00438243.2019.1617189.

Hamilakis, Y. (2014). *Archaeology and the Senses: Human Experience, Memory, and Affect.* Cambridge: Cambridge University Press.

Hamilakis, Y. & Infantidis, F. (2015). The photographic and the archaeological: The 'Other Acropolis'. In Carabott, P., Hamilakis, Y. & Papargyriou, E. (Eds.), *Camera Graeca: Photographs, Narratives, Materialities*, pp. 153–78. New York: Routledge.

Hamilakis, Y., Pluciennik, M. & Tarlow, S. (Eds.) (2002). *Thinking Through the Body: Archaeologies of Corporeality.* New York: Kluwer Academic.

Harris, O. J. (2017). Assemblages and scale in archaeology. *Cambridge Archaeological Journal* 27(1):127–39. https://doi.org/10.1017/S09597743 16000597.

Harris, O. J. (2021). Archaeology, process and time: Beyond history versus memory. *World Archaeology* 53(1):104–21. https://doi.org/10.1080/00438243 .2021.1963833.

Heyd, V. (2017). Kossinna's smile. *Antiquity* 91(356):348–59. https://doi.org/ 10.15184/aqy.2017.21.

Higuchi, R., Bowman, B., Freiberger, M., Ryder, O. A. & Wilson, A. C. (1984). DNA sequences from the quagga, an extinct member of the horse family. *Nature* 312(5991):282–4. https://doi.org/10.1038/312282a0.

Hodder, I. & Hutson, S. (2003). *Reading the Past: Current Approaches to Interpretation in Archaeology*. Cambridge: Cambridge University Press.

Holdaway, S. & Wandsnider, L. (Eds.) (2008). *Time in Archaeology: Time Perspectivism Revisited*. Salt Lake City: University of Utah Press.

Holst, M. K., Breuning-Madsen, H. & Rasmussen, M. (2001). The South Scandinavian barrows with well-preserved oak-log coffins. *Antiquity* 75:126–36. https://doi.org/10.1017/S0003598X00052820.

Holst, M. K. & Rasmussen, M. (2013). Herder communities: Longhouses, cattle and landscape organization in the Nordic Early and Middle Bronze Age. In Bergerbrant, S. & Sabatini, S. (Eds.), *Counterpoint: Essays in Archaeology and Heritage Studies in Honour of Professor Kristian Kristiansen*, pp. 99–110. International Series 2508. Oxford: British Archaeological Reports.

Honeychurch. W. & Makarewicz, C. A. (2016). The archaeology of pastoral nomadism. *Annual Review of Anthropology* 45:341–59. https://doi.org/ 10.1146/annurev-anthro-102215-095827.

Horster, M. & Hächler, N. (2021). *The Impact of the Roman Empire on Landscapes*. Leiden: Brill.

Hoskins, W. G. (1954). *The Making of the English Landscape*. London: Hodder & Stoughton.

Hu, L., Chartrand, M. M. G., St-Jean, G., Lopes, M. & Bataille, C. P. (2020). Assessing the reliability of mobility interpretation from a multi-isotope hair profile on a traveling individual. *Frontiers in Ecology and Evolution* 8:568943. https://doi.org/10.3389/fevo.2020.568943.

Ingold, T. (1993). The temporality of landscape. *World Archaeology* 25(2): 152–74. https://doi.org/10.1080/00438243.1993.9980235.

Ingold, T. (2000). *The Perception of the Environment: Essays on Livelihood, Dwelling and Skill*. London: Routledge.

Ingold, T. (2015). *The Life of Lines*. Oxford: Routledge.

Ingold, T. & Vergunst, J. L. (Eds.) (2016). *Ways of Walking: Ethnography and Practice on Foot*. London: Routledge.

Issartel, J.-L. (2008). L'exploitation touristique des grottes de Saint Marcel. In Faverjon, M., Brunet, P. & Dupré, B. (Eds.), *La Grotte de Saint Marcel d'Ardèche*, pp. 98–105. Chauzon: Comité Départemental de Spéléologie 07 Ardèche.

Jaillet, S. & Monney, J. (2018). Analyse 3D des volumes et remplissages souterrains de la grotte aux Points au temps des fréquentations paléolithiques (Aiguèze, Gard). *Karstologia* 72:27–36.

Jaubert, J., Verheyden, S., Genty, D., et al. (2016). Early Neanderthal constructions deep in Bruniquel Cave in southwestern France. *Nature* 534:111–4. https://doi.org/10.1038/nature18291.

Johnson, M. (2006). *Ideas of Landscape*. Oxford: Blackwell.

Kilhavn, H., Couchoud, I., Drysdale, R. N., et al. (2022). The 8.2 ka event in northern Spain: Timing, structure and climatic impact from a multi-proxy speleothem record. *EGUsphere* (preprint) https://doi.org/10.5194/egusphere-2022-386.

Knapp, A. B. (1992). Archaeology and Annales: Time, space, and change. In Knapp, A. B. (Ed.), *Archaeology, Annales, and Ethnohistory*, pp. 1–21. Cambridge: Cambridge University Press.

Knipper, C., Mitnick, A., Massy, K. & Stockhammer, P. (2017). Female exogamy and gene pool diversification at the transition from the final Neolithic to the Early Bronze Age in Central Europe. *Proceedings of the National Academy of Sciences* 114:10083–8. https://doi.org/10.1073/pnas.1706355114.

Knutson, S. A. (2020). Archaeology and the silk road model. *World Archaeology* 52(4):619–38. https://doi.org/10.1080/00438243.2021.1940268.

Kossinna, G. (1911). *Die Herkunft der Germanen: Zur Methode der Siedlungsarchäologie*. Würzburg: Kabitzsch.

Kristiansen, K. (2014). Towards a new paradigm: The third scientific revolution and its possible consequences in archaeology. *Current Swedish Archaeology* 22:11–34. https://doi.org/10.37718/CSA.2014.01.

Kristiansen, K. & Larsson, T. B. (2005). *The Rise of Bronze Age society: Travels, Transmissions and Transformations*. Cambridge: Cambridge University Press.

Kristiansen, K. & Suchowska-Ducke, P. (2015). Connected histories: The dynamics of Bronze Age interaction and trade 1500–1100 BC. *Proceedings of the Prehistoric Society* 81:361–92. https://doi.org/10.1017/ppr.2015.17.

Kristiansen, K., Allentoft, M.E., Frei, K. M., et al. (2017). Re-theorising mobility and the formation of culture and language among the Corded

Ware Culture in Europe. *Antiquity* 91(356):334–47. https://doi.org/10.15184/aqy.2017.17.

Kubler, G. (1962). *The Shape of Time: Remarks on the History of Things*. New Haven: Yale University Press.

Lacroix, D., Bell, T., Shaw, J. & Westley, K. (2014). Submerged archaeological landscapes and the recording of precontact history: Examples from Atlantic Canada. In Evans, A. M., Flatman, J. C. & Flemming, N. C. (Eds.), *Prehistoric Archaeology on the Continental Shelf*, pp. 13–35. New York: Springer.

Ladegaard-Pedersen, P., Sabatini, S., Frei, R., Kristiansen, K. & Frei, K. M. (2021). Testing Late Bronze Age mobility in southern Sweden in the light of a new multi-proxy strontium isotope baseline of Scania. *PLoS One* 16(4): e0250279. https://doi.org/10.1371/journal.pone.0250279.

LaMotta, V. & Schiffer, M. (2005). Archaeological formation processes. In Renfrew, C. & Bahn, P. (Eds.), *Archaeology: The Key Concepts*, pp. 121–7. New York: Routledge.

Laporte, L., Large, J.-M., Nespoulous, L., Scarre, C. & Steimer-Herbet, T. (Eds.) (2022). *Megaliths of the World Volume 1*. Oxford: Archaeopress.

Leveque, F. & Mora, P. (2021). The oldest Neanderthal fire deep in cave revealed by geomagnetic survey in Bruniquel Cave on the speleofacts structures covered by calcite concretions. In *AGU Fall Meeting Abstracts* December:GP51A-07. https://ui.adsabs.harvard.edu/abs/2021AGUFMGP51A..07L/abstract.

Lichter, M., Zviely, D., Klein, M. & Sivan, D. (2010). Sea-level changes in the Mediterranean: Past, present, and future – A review. In Israel, A., Einav, R. & Seckbach, J. (Eds.), *Seaweeds and Their Role in Globally Changing Environments*, pp. 3–17. Dordrecht: Springer.

Linse, A. R. (1993). Geoarchaeological scale and archaeological interpretation: Examples from the central Jornada Mogollon. In Stein, J. K. & Linse A. R. (Eds.), *Effects of Scale on Archaeological and Geoscientific Perspectives*, pp. 11–28. Special Paper 283. Boulder: Geological Society of America.

Lock, G. (Ed.) (2000). *Beyond the Map: Archaeology and Spatial Technologies*. Amsterdam: IOS Press.

Lourandos, H. (1996). Change in Australian prehistory: Scale, trends and frameworks of interpretation. In Ulm, S., Lilley I. & Ross, A. (Eds.), *Australian Archaeology '95: Proceedings of the 1995 Australian Archaeological Association Annual Conference*, pp. 15–21. St. Lucia: Anthropology Museum, University of Queensland.

Lucas, G. (2005). *The Archaeology of Time*. London: Routledge.

Lucas, G. (2021). *Making Time: The Archaeology of Time Revisited*. London: Routledge.

Madgwick, R., Lamb, A. L., Sloane, H., et al. (2019). Multi-isotope analysis reveals that feasts in the Stonehenge environs and across Wessex drew people and animals from throughout Britain. *Science Advances* 5(3):eaau6078. https://doi.org/10.1126/sciadv.aau6078.

Mafessoni, F., Grote, S., de Filippo, C., et al. (2020). A high-coverage Neandertal genome from Chagyrskaya Cave. *Proceedings of the National Academy of Sciences* 117(26):15132–6. https://doi.org/10.1073/pnas.20049 44117.

Maher, L. A. (2019). Persistent place-making in prehistory: The creation, maintenance, and transformation of an Epipalaeolithic landscape. *Journal of Archaeological Method and Theory* 26:998–1083. https://doi.org/10.1007/s10816-018-9403-1.

Mallery, G. (1893). *Picture-Writing of the American Indians*. Extract from the Tenth Annual Report of the Bureau of Ethnology, Smithsonian Institution, Washington D.C. https://library.si.edu/digital-library/book/picturewritingof 00mall.

Massy, K., Knipper, C., Mittnick, A., et al. (2017). Patterns of transformation from the Final Neolithic to the Early Bronze Age: A case study from the Lech Valley south of Augsburg. In Stockhammer, P. W. & Maran, J. (Eds.), *Appropriating Innovations: Entangled Knowledge in Eurasia, 5000–1500 BCE*, pp. 241–61. Oxford: Oxbow Books.

Mathieson, I., Lazaridis, I., Rohland, N., et al. (2015). Genome-wide patterns of selection in 230 ancient Eurasians. *Nature* 528:499–503. https://doi.org/10.1038/nature16152.

McFadyen, L. (2008). Building and architecture as landscape practice. In David, B. & Thomas, J. (Eds.), *Handbook of Landscape Archaeology*, pp. 307–14. Walnut Creek: Left Coast Press.

McGlade, J. (1999). The times of history: Archaeology, narrative and non-linear causality. In Murray, T. (Ed.), *Time and Archaeology*, pp. 139–63. London: Taylor & Francis.

Monney, J., Delannoy, J.-J., Geneste, J.-M., Jaillet, S. & Sadier, B. (2020). Les bassins topographiques. In Delannoy, J.-J. & Geneste, J.-M. (Eds.), *Monographie de la Grotte Chauvet-Pont d'Arc: Volume 1 – Atlas de la Grotte Chauvet-Pont d'Arc*, pp. 106–8. Paris: Documents de l'Archéologie Française, Éditions de la Maison des Sciences de l'Homme.

Montelle, Y.-P. (2022). The skull chamber in the Chauvet Cave: En route towards a theatre. *TDR: The Drama Review* 66(2):10–26. https://muse.jhu.edu/article/858113 N1.

Moran, M. (2020). 'Mehtaqtek, where the path comes to an end': Documenting cultural landscapes of movement in Wolastoqiyik (Maliseet) First Nation territory in New Brunswick, Canada, and Maine, United States. Unpublished PhD Thesis, College of William & Mary, Williamsburg.

Murray, T. (2008). Paradigms and metaphysics, or 'Is this the end of archaeology as we know it?'. In Holdaway, S. & Wandsnider, L. (Eds.), *Time in Archaeology: Time Perspectivism Revisited*, pp. 171–80. Salt Lake City: University of Utah Press.

Murrieta-Flores, P. A. (2010). Travelling in a prehistoric landscape: Exploring the influences that shaped human movement. In Frischer, B., Crawford, J. W. & Koller, D. (Eds.), *Making History Interactive: Computer Applications and Quantitative Methods in Archaeology (CAA) – Proceedings of the 37th International Conference (Williamsburg, Virginia, United States of America 2009)*, pp. 258–76. International Series 2079. Oxford: British Archaeological Reports.

Olalde, I., Brace, S., Allentoft, M. E., et al. (2018). The Beaker phenomenon and the genomic transformation of northwest Europe. *Nature* 555(7695): 190–6. https://doi.org/10.1038/nature25738.

Olive, M. & Vanrell, L. (2021). La caverne et ses différents espaces. In Vanrell, L. & Olive, M. (Eds.), *La Grotte Cosquer: Trente Ans de Recherches. Dossiers d'Archéologie* 408:26–9.

Ontañón, R. (2003). Sols et structures d'habitat du Paléolithique supérieur, nouvelles données depuis les Cantabres: La Galerie Inférieure de La Garma (Cantabria, Espagne). *L'Anthropologie* 107(3):333–63. https://doi.org/10.1016/S0003-5521(03)00037-2.

Pääbo, S. (1985). Molecular cloning of ancient Egyptian mummy DNA. *Nature* 314(6012):644–5. https://doi.org/10.1038/314644a0.

Pearson, M. P., Pollard, J., Richards, C., Thomas, J., Tilley, C. & Welham, K. (2020). *Stonehenge for the Ancestors: Part 1 – Landscape and Monuments*. Leiden: Sidestone Press.

Perrette, Y., Delannoy, J.-J., Bolvin, H., et al. (2000). Comparative study of a stalagmite sample by stratigraphy, laser induced fluorescence spectroscopy, EPR spectrometry and reflectance imaging. *Chemical Geology* 162(3–4): 221–43. https://doi.org/10.1016/S0009-2541(99)00069-8.

Perrette, Y., Delannoy, J.-J., Desmet, M., Lignier, V. & Destombes, J. L. (2005). Speleothem organic matter content imaging: The use of a Fluorescence Index to characterise the maximum emission wavelength.

Chemical Geology 214(3–4):193–208. https://doi.org/10.1016/j.chemgeo .2004.09.002.

Price, T. D. (2014). An introduction to the isotopic studies of ancient human remains. *Journal of the North Atlantic* (Special Volume 7):71–87. www.jstor .org/stable/26671846.

Quiers, M., Perrette, Y., Chalmin, E., Fanget, B. & Poulenard, J. (2015). Geochemical mapping of organic carbon in stalagmites using liquid-phase and solid-phase fluorescence. *Chemical Geology* 411:240–7. https://doi.org/ 10.1016/j.chemgeo.2015.07.012.

Quiles, A., Valladas, H., Bocherens, H., et al. (2016). A high-precision chrono-logical model for the decorated Upper Paleolithic cave of Chauvet-Pont d'Arc, Ardèche, France. *Proceedings of the National Academy of Sciences of the United States of America* 113(17):4670–5. https://doi.org/10.1073/ pnas.1523158113.

Rasmussen, M., Li, T., Lindgreen, S., et al. (2010). Ancient human genome sequence of an extinct Paleo-Eskimo. *Nature* 463:757–62. https://doi.org/ 10.1038/nature08835.

Raymond, W. O. (1910). *The River St. John, Its Physical Features, Legends and History from 1604–1784*. St. John, N. B.: John A. Bowes. https://archive.org/ details/riverstjohnitsph00raym/page/63/mode/1up?view=theater.

Reid, J. J., Schiffer, M. & Rathje, W. L. (1975). Behavioral archaeology: Four strategies. *American Anthropologist* 77(4):864–9. www.jstor.org/stable/ 674794.

Reiter, S. S., Frei, K. M., Nørgaard, H. W. & Kaul, F. (2019). The Ølby Woman: A comprehensive provenance investigation of an elite Nordic Bronze Age oak-coffin burial. *Danish Journal of Archaeology* 8:1–22. https://doi.org/ 10.7146/dja.v8i0.114995.

Renes, J. (2015). Layered landscapes: A problematic theme in historic land-scape research. In Kolen, J., Renes, J. & Hermans, R. (Eds.), *Landscape Biographies*, pp. 403–21. Amsterdam: Amsterdam University Press.

Renfrew, C. (1972). *The Emergence of Civilization: The Cyclades and the Aegean in the Third Millennium*. London: Methuen.

Renfrew, C. (1981). Space, time and man. *Transactions of the Institute of British Geographers* 6:257–78. https://doi.org/10.2307/622287.

Rouzaud, F., Soulier, M. & Lignereux, Y. (1995). La grotte de Bruniquel. *Spelunca* 60:27–34.

Sadier, B., Benedetti, L., Bourlès, D. L., Delannoy, J.-J. & Jaillet, S. (2020). Datation ^{36}Cl de la paroi extérieure et du porche préhistorique. In Delannoy, J.-J. & Geneste, J.-M. (Eds.), *Monographie de la Grotte Chauvet-Pont d'Arc: Volume 1 – Atlas de la Grotte Chauvet-Pont d'Arc*, pp. 130–2.

Paris: Documents de l'Archéologie Française, Éditions de la Maison des Sciences de l'Homme.

Sadier, B., Delannoy, J.-J., Benedetti, L., et al. (2012). Further constraints on the Chauvet Cave artwork elaboration. *Proceedings of the National Academy of Sciences of the United States of America* 109(21):8002–6. https://doi.org/ 10.1073/pnas.1118593109.

Sanger, D. (1975). Culture change as an adaptive process in the Maine-Maritimes region. *Arctic Anthropology* 12(2):60–75. www.jstor.org/ stable/40315875.

Schama, S. (1995). *Landscape and Memory.* New York: A. A. Knopf.

Schiffer, M. B. (1976). *Behavioral Archaeology.* New York: Academic Press.

Schiffer, M. B. (1985). Is there a 'Pompeii Premise' in archaeology? *Journal of Anthropological Research* 41(1):18–41. https://doi.org/10.1086/jar.41.1 .3630269.

Schiffer, M. B. (1987). *Formation Processes of the Archaeological Record.* Albuquerque: University of New Mexico Press.

Schlanger, S. H. (1992). Recognizing persistent places in Anasazi settlement systems. In Rossignol, J. & Wandsnider, L. (Eds.), *Space, Time, and Archaeological Landscapes: Interdisciplinary Contributions to Archaeology,* pp. 91–112. Boston: Springer. https://doi.org/10.1007/978-1-4899-2450-6_5.

Shaw, A., Bates, M., Conneller, C., et al. (2016). The archaeology of persistent places: The Palaeolithic case of La Cotte de St Brelade, Jersey. *Antiquity* 90(354):1437–53. https://doi.org/10.15184/aqy.2016.212.

Simiand, F. (1903). Méthode historique et science sociale. *Review* 9(1985– 1986):163–213. www.persee.fr/doc/ahess_0395-2649_1960_num_15_1_ 421747.

Simón Vallejo, M. D., Parrilla Giráldez, R., Macías Tejada, S., Calle Román, L., Mayoral Valsera, J. & Cortés Sánchez, L. M. (2021). Cueva de La Pileta y las representaciones de manos en el arte paleolítico del sur de Iberia. In Bea, M., Domingo, R., Mazo, C., Montes, L. & Rodanés, J. M. (Eds.), *De la Mano de la Prehistoria: Homenaje a Pilar Utrilla Miranda*, pp. 97–108. Zaragoza: Prensas de la Universidad de Zaragoza.

Skousen, J. (2018). Rethinking archaeologies of pilgrimage. *Journal of Social Archaeology* 18(30):261–83. https://doi.org/10.1177/1469605318763626.

Slon, V., Hopfe, C., Weiß, C. L., et al. (2017). Neandertal and Denisovan DNA from Pleistocene sediments. *Science* 356(6338):605–8. www.science.org/ doi/10.1126/science.aam9695.

Stewart, A. M., Keith, D. & Scottie, J. (2004). Caribou crossings and cultural meanings: Placing traditional knowledge and archaeological context in an

Inuit landscape. *Journal of Archaeological Method and Theory* 11(2): 183–211. https://doi.org/10.1023/B:JARM.0000038066.09898.cd.

Stockhammer, P. W., Massy, K., Knipper, C., et al. (2015). Rewriting the Central European Early Bronze Age chronology: Evidence from large-scale radiocarbon dating. *PLoS ONE* 10(10):e0139705. https://doi.org/10.1371/journal.pone.0139705.

Suttie, B. (2003). Final Report: 1997 Bentley Street Site (BhDm2) Test Excavations. Unpublished report on file, Archaeological and Heritage Services Branch, Government of New Brunswick, Fredericton.

Suttie, B. & Allen, P. (2015). Bentley Street Archaeological Site. In *The Canadian Encyclopedia*. www.thecanadianencyclopedia.ca/en/article/bentley-street-archaeological-site.

Supernant, K. (2022). Archaeology sits in places. *Journal of Anthropological Archaeology* 66:101416. https://doi.org/10.1016/j.jaa.2022.101416.

Sykes, N., Spriggs, M. & Evin, A. (2019). Beyond curse or blessing: The opportunities and challenges of aDNA analyses. *World Archaeology* 51(4): 503–16. https://doi.org/10.1080/00438243.2019.1741970.

Theunissen, R., Balme, J. & Beck, W. (1998). Headroom and human trampling: Cave ceiling-height determines the spatial patterning of stone artefacts at Petzkes Cave, northern New South Wales. *Antiquity* 72:80–89.

Thomas, J. (2008). Archaeology, landscape, and dwelling. In David, B. & Thomas, J. (Eds.), *Handbook of Landscape Archaeology*, pp. 300–6. Walnut Creek: Left Coast Press.

Thomsen, E. & Andreasen, R. (2019). Agricultural lime disturbs natural strontium isotope variations: Implications for provenance and migration studies. *Science Advances* 5:eaav8083:1–11. www.science.org/doi/10.1126/sciadv.aav8083.

Thomsen, E., Andreasen, R. & Rasmussen, T. L. (2021). Homogeneous glacial landscapes can have high local variability of strontium isotope signatures: Implications for prehistoric migration studies. *Frontiers in Ecology and Evolution* 8:588318:1–18. https://doi.org/10.3389/fevo.2020.588318.

Thomson, D. F. (1939). The seasonal factor in human culture illustrated from the life of a contemporary nomadic group. *Proceedings of the Prehistoric Society* 5(2):209–21. https://doi.org/10.1017/S0079497X00020545.

Tilley, C. (2008). Phenomenological approaches to landscape archaeology. In David, B. & Thomas, J. (Eds.), *Handbook of Landscape Archaeology*, pp. 271–6. London: Routledge.

Tipple, B. J., Valenzuela, L.O. & Ehleringer, J. R. (2018). Strontium isotope ratios of human hair record intra-city variations in tap water source. *Scientific Reports* 8(1):1–10. https://doi.org/10.1038/s41598-018-21359-0.

Urwin, C., David, B., Delannoy, J.-J., Bell, J. A. & Geneste, J.-M. (2022). Aboriginal monumental stone-working in northern Australia during the Pleistocene. In Laporte, L., Large, J.-M., Nespoulous, L., Scarre, C. & Steimer-Herbet, T. (Eds.), *Megaliths of the World* Volume 1, pp. 241–55. Oxford: Archaeopress.

Valladas, H., Bocherens, H., Bon, C., et al. (2020d). Datation ^{14}C des ossements. In Delannoy, J.-J. & Geneste, J.-M. (Eds.), *Monographie de la Grotte Chauvet-Pont d'Arc: Volume 1 – Atlas de la Grotte Chauvet-Pont d'Arc*, p. 125. Paris: Documents de l'Archéologie Française, Éditions de la Maison des Sciences de l'Homme.

Valladas, H., Quiles, A., Delannoy, J.-J., et al. (2020a). Introduction. In Delannoy, J.-J. & Geneste, J.-M. (Eds.), *Monographie de la Grotte Chauvet-Pont d'Arc: Volume 1 – Atlas de la Grotte Chauvet-Pont d'Arc*, pp. 119–20. Paris: Documents de l'Archéologie Française, Éditions de la Maison des Sciences de l'Homme.

Valladas, H., Quiles, A., Delqué-Količ, E., et al. (2020b). Datation ^{14}C des charbons du sol. In Delannoy, J.-J. & Geneste, J.-M. (Eds.), *Monographie de la Grotte Chauvet-Pont d'Arc: Volume 1 – Atlas de la Grotte Chauvet-Pont d'Arc*, pp. 121–2. Paris: Documents de l'Archéologie Française, Éditions de la Maison des Sciences de l'Homme.

Valladas, H., Quiles, A., Delqué-Količ, E., et al. (2020c). Datation ^{14}C des tracés pariétaux. In Delannoy, J.-J. & Geneste, J.-M. (Eds.), *Monographie de la Grotte Chauvet-Pont d'Arc: Volume 1 – Atlas de la Grotte Chauvet-Pont d'Arc*, pp. 123–4. Paris: Documents de l'Archéologie Française, Éditions de la Maison des Sciences de l'Homme.

Valladas, H., Quiles, A., Delque-Kolic, M., et al. (2017). Radiocarbon dating of the decorated Cosquer Cave (France). *Radiocarbon* 59(2):621–33. https://doi.org/10.1017/RDC.2016.87.

Van der Merwe, N. J. & Vogel, J. C. (1978). ^{13}C content of human collagen as a measure of prehistoric diet in woodland North America. *Nature* 276:815–6. https://doi.org/10.1038/276815a0.

Vandevelde, S., Brochier, J. É., Desachy, B., Petit, C. & Slimak, L. (2018). Sooted concretions: A new micro-chronological tool for high temporal resolution archaeology. *Quaternary International* 474, Part B:103–18. https://doi.org/10.1016/j.quaint.2017.10.031.

Vandevelde, S., Brochier, J. É., Petit, C. & Slimak, L. (2017). Establishment of occupation chronicles in Grotte Mandrin using sooted concretions: Rethinking the Middle to Upper Paleolithic transition. *Journal of Human Evolution* 112:70–8. https://doi.org/10.1016/j.jhevol.2017.07.016.

Vandevelde, S., Genty, D., Brochier, J. É., Petit, C. & Slimak, L. (2020). Des concrétions fuligineuses en contextes archéologiques: Quel potentiel informatif? *Géomorphologie: Relief, Processus, Environnement* 26(4):241–54. https://doi.org/10.4000/geomorphologie.14981.

Van Dyke, R. M. (2018). From enchantment to *agencement*: Archaeological engagements with pilgrimage. *Journal of Social Archaeology* 18(3):348–59. https://doi.org/10.1177/1469605318773846.

Vanrell, L. & Olive, M. (2021a). Les datations des oeuvres de la grotte Cosquer. In Vanrell, L. & Olive, M. (Eds.), *La Grotte Cosquer: Trente Ans de Recherches. Dossiers d'Archéologie* 408:30–7.

Vanrell, L. & Olive, M. (2021b). L'art pariétal de la grotte Cosquer. In Vanrell, L. & Olive, M. (Eds.), *La Grotte Cosquer: Trente Ans de Recherches. Dossiers d'Archéologie* 408:38–47.

Vavouranakis, G. (2015). Time past and time present: The emergence of the Minoan palace as a transformation of temporality. In Polychroniadis, Z. T. & Evely, D. (Eds.), *Aegis: Essays in Mediterranean Archaeology Presented to Matti Egon*, pp. 35–43. Oxford: Archaeopress.

Verheyden, S., Jaubert, J., Genty, D., et al. (2016). Geo-archaeological study of a broken stalagmite structure in the Bruniquel Cave, Tarn-et-Garonne, France. In Baele, J.-M., Papier, S., Devleeschouwer, X., Dupont, N., Goderniaux, P., Michel Hennebert, M. & Kaufmann, O. (Eds.), *5th International Geologica Belgica Congress: 26–29 January 2016 – Geologica Belgica Conference Proceedings* Volume 2, p. 147. Mons: University of Mons. https://doi.org/10.20341/gbcp.vol2.

Vernot, B., Zavala, E. I., Gómez-Olivencia, A., et al. (2021). Unearthing Neanderthal population history using nuclear and mitochondrial DNA from cave sediments. *Science* 372(6542):p.eabf1667. www.science.org/doi/10.1126/science.abf1667.

Ward, I. & Larcombe, P. (2020). Sedimentary unknowns constrain the current use of frequency analysis of radiocarbon data sets in forming regional models of demographic change. *Geoarchaeology* 36(3):546–70. https://doi.org/10.1002/gea.21837.

Witmore, C. (2007). Landscape, time, topology: An archaeological account of the southern Argolid, Greece. In Hicks, D., McAtackney, L. & Fairclough, G. (Eds.), *Envisioning Landscape: Situations and Standpoints in Archaeology and Heritage*, pp. 194–225. Walnut Creek: Taylor & Francis Group.

Witcher, R. (1998). Roman roads: Phenomenological perspectives on roads in the landscape. In Forcery, C., Hawthorne, J. & Witcher, T. (Eds.), *Proceedings of the Seventh Annual Theoretical Roman Archaeology Conference, Nottingham 1997*, pp. 60–70. Oxford: Oxbow Books.

Wright, E., Viner-Daniels, S., Pearson, M. P. & Albarella, U. (2014). Age and season of pig slaughter at Late Neolithic Durrington Walls (Wiltshire, UK) as detected through a new system for recording tooth wear. *Journal of Archaeological Science* 52:497–514. https://doi.org/10.1016/j.jas.2014 .09.009.

Wylie, A. (1989). Archaeological cables and tacking: The implications of practice for Bernstein's 'Options beyond Objectivism and Relativism'. *Philosophy of the Social Sciences* 19:1–18.

Acknowledgements

We offer our deepest thanks to Bruno Arfib (Centre Européen de Recherche et d'enseignement des Géosciences de l'environment (CEREGE), Centre National de la Recherche Scientifique (CNRS)-Université Aix-Marseille, France), Lucilla Benedetti (CEREGE, CNRS-Université Aix-Marseille, France), Stéphane Jaillet (Laboratoire Environnements, Dynamiques et Territoires de Montagne (EDYTEM)-CNRS, France), Jules Kemper (EDYTEM-Université Savoie Mont Blanc, France), Irene Schimmelpfennig (CEREGE, CNRS-Université Aix-Marseille, France), Ségolène Vandevelde (Laboratoire des Sciences du Climat et de l'Environment (CEA), CNRS-Université Paris 1 Panthéon-Sorbonne, France), and Luc Vanrell (Laboratoire Méditerranéen de Préhistoire Europe et Afrique (LAMPEA-CNRS)-Université Aix-Marseille, France), each of whom kindly read through individual sections, made invaluable comments that enabled us to refine both our ideas and the details presented in this Element, and/or supplied Supplementary Information or figures. We are very grateful also to GunaiKurnai Elder Russell Mullett and Joanna Fresløv for the many discussions and wise words, by which we constantly reflect on what we write and how we write it: thank you so much for your friendship, discussions, advice and feedback. Many thanks to Joanna Fresløv for commenting on the whole Element, and to Hans Barnard for inviting us to write it in the first place.

Thank you to the GunaiKurnai Land and Waters Aboriginal Corporation for continued support and for permission to discuss and include previously unpublished photos of Cloggs Cave and other parts of GunaiKurnai Country. We also thank the New Brunswick Museum – Musée Nouveau Brunswick for collegial support and permission to publish images from their archival collections.

For institutional support we thank the Monash Indigenous Studies Centre at Monash University (Australia), the Centre for Ancient Cultures at Monash University (Australia), the Australian Research Council Centre of Excellence for Australian Biodiversity and Heritage (CABAH), the Laboratoire EDYTEM and CNRS at the Université Savoie-Mont Blanc (France), Ministère de la Culture (France), Cuevas Prehistoricas de Cantabria (Cueva de La Garma, Spain), and Grotte de Saint Marcel d'Ardèche (France).

Cambridge Elements ≡

Current Archaeological Tools and Techniques

Hans Barnard

University of California, Los Angeles

Hans Barnard is an Associate Adjunct Professor in the Department of Near Eastern Languages and Cultures at the University of California, Los Angeles, as well as an Associate Researcher at the Cotsen Institute of Archaeology.

Willeke Wendrich

University of California, Los Angeles

Willeke Wendrich is the Joan Silsbee Chair of African Cultural Archaeology and the Director of the Cotsen Institute of Archaeology at UCLA. In addition she is Professor of Egyptian Archaeology and Digital Humanities in the Department of Near Eastern Languages and Cultures at the University of California, Los Angeles as well as the Editor-in-Chief of the online UCLA Encyclopedia of Egyptology.

About the Series

Cambridge University Press and the Cotsen Institute of Archaeology at UCLA collaborate on this series of Elements, which aims to facilitate deployment of specific techniques by archaeologists in the field and in the laboratory. It provides readers with a basic understanding of selected techniques, followed by clear instructions how to implement them, or how to collect samples to be analyzed by a third party, and how to approach interpretation of the results.

COTSEN INSTITUTE OF
ARCHAEOLOGY AT UCLA

Cambridge Elements ⁼

Current Archaeological Tools and Techniques

Printed in the United States
by Baker & Taylor Publisher Services